THE BEDFORD SERIES IN HISTORY AND CULTURE

Common Sense

AND RELATED WRITINGS

by Thomas Paine

Related Titles in
THE BEDFORD SERIES IN HISTORY AND CULTURE
Advisory Editors: Natalie Zemon Davis, Princeton University
Ernest R. May, Harvard University
David W. Blight, Amherst College

THE BEDFORD SERIES IN HISTORY AND CULTURE

Common Sense

AND RELATED WRITINGS

by Thomas Paine

Edited with an Introduction by

Thomas P. Slaughter

Rutgers University

BEDFORD/ST. MARTIN'S   Boston ♦ New York

Dedicated to Philip Greven and John Murrin — mentors in many ways

For Bedford/St. Martin's
Executive Editor for History: Katherine E. Kurzman
Developmental Editor: Molly E. Kalkstein
Senior Production Supervisor: Cheryl Mamaril
Project Management: Books By Design, Inc.
Text Design: Claire Seng-Niemoeller
Indexer: Books By Design, Inc.
Cover Design: Richard Emery
Cover Art: Thomas Paine by W. Sharp, 1793. Engraving after a painting by George Romney. © Collection of the New-York Historical Society.
Composition: Stratford Publishing Services
Printing and Binding: Haddon Craftsmen, an R. R. Donnelley & Sons Company

President: Charles H. Christensen
Editorial Director: Joan E. Feinberg
Director of Marketing: Karen R. Melton
Director of Editing, Design, and Production: Marcia Cohen
Manager, Publishing Services: Emily Berleth

Library of Congress Control Number: 00-104953

Manufactured in the United States of America.

6 5 4 3 2 1
f e d c b a

For information, write: Bedford/St. Martin's, 75 Arlington Street, Boston, MA 02116
(617-399-4000)

ISBN: 0-312-20148-6 (paperback)
0-312-23704-9 (hardcover)

Foreword

The Bedford Series in History and Culture is designed so that readers can study the past as historians do.

The historian's first task is finding the evidence. Documents, letters, memoirs, interviews, pictures, movies, novels, or poems can provide facts and clues. Then the historian questions and compares the sources. There is more to do than in a courtroom, for hearsay evidence is welcome, and the historian is usually looking for answers beyond act and motive. Different views of an event may be as important as a single verdict. How a story is told may yield as much information as what it says.

Along the way the historian seeks help from other historians and perhaps from specialists in other disciplines. Finally, it is time to write, to decide on an interpretation and how to arrange the evidence for readers.

Each book in this series contains an important historical document or group of documents, each document a witness from the past and open to interpretation in different ways. The documents are combined with some element of historical narrative—an introduction or a biographical essay, for example—that provides students with an analysis of the primary source material and important background information about the world in which it was produced.

Each book in the series focuses on a specific topic within a specific historical period. Each provides a basis for lively thought and discussion about several aspects of the topic and the historian's role. Each is short enough (and inexpensive enough) to be a reasonable one-week assignment in a college course. Whether as classroom or personal reading, each book in the series provides firsthand experience of the challenge—and fun—of discovering, recreating, and interpreting the past.

Natalie Zemon Davis
Ernest R. May
David W. Blight

Preface

Common Sense is the centerpiece of this collection of Thomas Paine's writings. There are a number of ways of presenting this pamphlet to a student audience, but this one places it in the context of Paine's other writings that immediately preceded and followed *Common Sense*.

This approach is based on the premise that the pivotal influence on Thomas Paine was his perception of America during the year prior to writing and publishing *Common Sense*. The introduction invites you to look to Paine's childhood and youth for the plausible origins of his passionate opposition to social injustice. You may consider the proximity of Paine's birthplace to his town's execution site, for example, as a formative influence on his social conscience, and look to the corruption of local government as a source of his disdain for the actual, as opposed to Americans' romantically theoretical, British Constitution. The introduction postulates Paine's childhood spent on the "Wilderness" heath as an early source for the naturalism permeating *Common Sense*. It also helps to identify the pull of Paine's parents' two religions—Quakerism and Anglicanism—as a source for his apparently contradictory attitudes toward the Bible and organized religion. In Paine's artisanal roots we find a primitive mold of his class perspective on society and politics. And, finally, the introduction similarly considers Paine's failures as a young adult, both romantically and professionally, as influences on his writings.

The biographical background in the introduction gives less attention to the possible literary influences on Paine's writing than is typically the case. This is because every effort to locate the intellectual pedigree of *Common Sense* in written texts has failed. There is absolutely no evidence that Paine read any of the political tracts associated with the ideological origins of the American Revolution. The ideas of *Common Sense* are in significant ways at odds with those of John Locke, the seventeenth-century English political philosopher; John Trenchard and Thomas Gordon, the early eighteenth-century English political writers popularly known as the "Real Whigs"; and the French Enlightenment philosophers Jean-Jacques Rousseau and Montesquieu. The influences of these men on Paine have been variously asserted, contested, denied, and disproved.

Instead, this edition celebrates Thomas Paine's creativity, the novelty of *Common Sense,* and the fact that Paine's style, more than the pamphlet's content, accounts for its huge success. Paine's place in the history of propaganda and the wider history of dramatic writing are emphasized here. His ability to move people emotionally was Paine's essential genius and requires greater explication than his ideas, which are both commonplace and inconsistently applied. Paine was not a great thinker and *Common Sense* is not a great work of political philosophy. Paine was, though, the great political propagandist of the American Revolution, and *Common Sense* is one of the most influential pieces of political literature ever written in the English language.

Of the eight works included here, five are from Paine's 1775 American writings. I chose them for their own qualities and because they show him working out some of the writing style and themes that he honed for *Common Sense.* They reveal him at work on his craft and engaged with public issues—slavery, the slave trade, the "occupation" of America by British troops, and justification for defensive war—that remained central to the enterprise of the following year. We see also, in Paine's essay on marriage, some of the private issues that impelled him to become an American and the assumptions about the moral and emotional makeup of human beings that are at the heart of his skill as a pamphleteer. The 1775 writings, in sum, serve as a bridge between Paine's earlier life and his most influential work. They help us understand who he was and who he would become.

Likewise, the two other 1776 writings included in addition to *Common Sense* play out the events of that incredible year and Paine's role in both inspiring and sustaining the Revolution through its darkest times. The first of his "Forester" letters responds to critics of *Common Sense,* defends the pamphlet and the war effort, and pushes forward his methods and plans. The first in Paine's series on *The American Crisis* was as important in sustaining the war effort at a critical time as *Common Sense* had been in inspiring it, and was as emotionally appealing as any writing that Paine ever did.

This, then, is the essential Thomas Paine of the American Revolutionary era. This is the inspiring literary figure of the war's first year. This is the Thomas Paine who addressed the hearts of common people, providing necessary fervor for what he made a moral cause. These are the writings that every American must engage if we are to comprehend our revolutionary roots as part of a historical process that moved people to act and that scared some of the Founding Fathers by their appeal to higher democratic ideals, deep passions, and an open-eyed look at the social tensions that the Revolution would not resolve.

ACKNOWLEDGMENTS

Students in my undergraduate class on the American Revolution convinced me that Thomas Paine's writings are essential to their understanding of the events of 1776 and that we needed an introduction to Paine and his writings that explains more about him and fabricates less about the intellectual lineage of *Common Sense*. This volume, then, is my attempt to answer their questions and to place one of the great works of English literature and American politics within personal and authorial contexts that make sense to me and, I hope, to those who read it. I am most grateful to the students who have asked the questions, challenged the answers, and picked apart other people's introductions to Paine's writings.

My association with the David Library of the American Revolution, in Washington's Crossing, Pennsylvania, over the past decade has also helped me focus on the challenges associated with presenting the Revolution to audiences of interested people who are not all academic historians. As a member of the library's advisory board and board of trustees, I have come to appreciate just how difficult it is to run such an operation, how important a service such places provide, and how hard it can be to communicate the complexity of the American Revolution without oversimplifying or mythologizing our history. I thank David Fowler, the library's director, and Marjorie Torango, president of the library's board of trustees, for their hard work in a noble cause.

Katherine Kurzman convinced me that I should do something for the Bedford Series in History and Culture. I thank her for her confidence and patience. Without her persistence, I would have missed this opportunity to take on Thomas Paine. Molly Kalkstein, this volume's editor, has improved the content, smoothed the process, and hastened its completion, all of which are to its and my benefit. Also at Bedford/St. Martin's, Heidi Hood started the editorial process rolling, Zenobia Rivetna supervised the design of the cover, and Emily Berleth was production manager. At Books By Design, Nancy Benjamin was the project editor.

I also thank the readers who gave the volume careful readings and provided helpful suggestions. Lance Banning, John Demos, Ronald Schultz, James Roger Sharp, Rebecca S. Shoemaker, Billy G. Smith, and Rosemarie Zagarri were model reviewers. Having never met most of them, and knowing the rest mainly through their work, I greatly appreciate their generosity and support for this project.

The dedication acknowledges a more general and longer-term debt to my graduate school mentor, John M. Murrin, and my Rutgers colleague Philip J. Greven. The coincidence of their simultaneous retirements and the publication of this book reminds me at my mid-career of their generosity, encouragement, and support. I remain forever grateful.

Thomas P. Slaughter

A Note about the Texts

The five essays written by Paine during 1775 that are included here are from the *Pennsylvania Journal* and are reprinted in Moncure Daniel Conway's *The Writings of Thomas Paine,* 2 vols. (New York: G. P. Putnam's Sons, 1894).

The first edition of *Common Sense* was printed by Richard Bell on January 10, 1776. The next was an expanded edition printed by William Bradford on February 14, 1776. The demand for the pamphlet was so great that Bradford subcontracted the printing to two firms, Melchior Styner and Charles Cist, and Benjamin Towne. Towne's was the more accurate of the two and is the one used here.

The four Forester letters appeared in several Philadelphia newspapers. The first printing of "Letter I. To Cato" was in the *Pennsylvania Packet,* April 1, 1776. That is the text reprinted here.

The American Crisis, Number 1, appeared first in pamphlet form and was later widely reprinted in newspapers. The first publication was by Styner and Cist on December 19, 1776. A second printing by the same firm followed shortly thereafter. The pamphlet was reprinted numerous times and thousands of copies circulated during the war.

Contents

Illustrations

THE BEDFORD SERIES IN HISTORY AND CULTURE

Common Sense

AND RELATED WRITINGS

by Thomas Paine

PART ONE

Introduction:
Thomas Paine's America

Thomas Paine was a man of science, an inventor of a single-span iron bridge, a philosopher of religion as concerned with God's realm as he was with human arenas, and a propagandist for political change. His fame is rightly based on his writings; his literary talents were inspirational, evoking emotions in his readers more effectively than any other writer of his day. Paine's true genius, however, was as a revolutionary. He was a brilliant writer of short works—pamphlets, newspaper essays, and public letters—on the events of the moment. He played an inspiring role in both the American and French revolutions at critical early stages and helped to sustain, again principally with his pen, the American cause through a long and brutal war.

Paine's essential contribution to the American Revolution came during the first year of the war, when he wrote *Common Sense* and the first of his *American Crisis* essays. It would be difficult to overstate the significance of *Common Sense* in creating support for the war effort, or of the *Crisis* essays in sustaining it through the darkest days of the conflict. It would be impossible to understand the origins of this nation without addressing Paine's revolutionary prose, which at once captured the high emotional drama of the political scene and inspired countless thousands to fight against the most powerful military force in the world.

Common Sense hit Philadelphia like a thunderclap on a calm day. It startled people. It scared some, thrilled others, and enraged quite a

1

few. The emotional impact of the pamphlet is difficult for us to appreciate, because written words no longer have such incendiary power. In our modern world electronic images ignite the cultural flames that engulf us; entertainment—sports, music, and film—has supplanted politics and religion as the theatrical center of public life.

It is hard for us to imagine so many people becoming so aroused by the words printed in one little pamphlet. Yet Thomas Paine's words encouraged them to risk all that they held dear—their lives, their livelihoods, their property, and those whom they loved—in a war against the most formidable military power in the world. And for what—for ephemeral concepts like freedom and equality, when they already lived, as they well knew, in the most free and equal society in the recorded history of the Western world. Yet they did just that; they risked all because they believed, as *Common Sense* told them, that there was no better time than the present to declare their independence from the past and take charge of their future. "'Tis time to part," Paine proclaimed. Americans went to war because they shared the values, fears, sensibilities, and ambitions that *Common Sense* articulated so clearly, so powerfully, and so convincingly. They took up arms because they, like Paine, believed that "the sun never shined on a cause of greater worth" (p. 86 in this volume). Because *Common Sense* tapped into this collective consciousness of what it meant to be an American, and because it moved so many to act, it is essential that we try to comprehend the pamphlet's impact if we are to understand the origins of our nation and the enduring legacy of the American Revolution.

To fully appreciate the place of *Common Sense* in the American Revolution and the creation of a distinctively American political culture, we need to understand the man who wrote it. We will explore briefly the influences and experiences that helped make Thomas Paine the most effective political propagandist of his day. We will examine why he felt so passionately about his political ideals. We will learn what brought him to America and led him to the forefront of the Revolutionary movement in the brief period of one year that he was in Philadelphia before writing *Common Sense*.

With that in mind, five of the essays that Paine wrote during 1775 are included here. In March and October, Paine published essays denouncing slavery and advocating an end to the slave trade. In January and July, he published essays opposing the British military occupation of America and advocating defensive war against them if British troops refused to withdraw. In June, his essay on unhappy marriages appeared. Here we will see Paine's past life connecting with his new start in America. We will also see how Paine's stylistic and thematic developments helped make *Common Sense* so distinctive. After *Common Sense,* Paine continued to write in support of the American Revolution. He wrote four essays, which he signed "The Forester," in defense of *Common Sense* and the Revolutionary movement. The first of these is included here. He also wrote a series of ten essays between 1776 and 1780 entitled *The American Crisis.* The first of these *Crisis* essays is among Paine's most significant writings; it is included here because it had a profound impact on the Revolutionary War and bears some striking stylistic similarities to *Common Sense.*

Our principal focus, though, will remain *Common Sense,* which is one of the most important pieces of political literature ever written in the English language. Ultimately, we need to consider the pamphlet on both eighteenth-century terms and our own as a reflection of the ways that the past affects the present and connects to the future.

YOUNG TOM PAINE

Thomas Paine[1] first opened his eyes in Thetford, England, during the winter of 1737. His mother, Frances (Cocke) Pain, who was the daughter of an attorney, was forty years old when she gave birth to her son. She was baptized an Anglican and practiced this religion throughout her long life. She and Thomas's father, Joseph Pain, married on June 20, 1734. Frances was eleven years older than her husband. Her second child, a daughter, was born about eighteen months after Thomas, but died in infancy. Paine's first biographer, who interviewed neighbors of the Pain family, described Thomas's mother as "a woman of sour temper and an eccentric character." Whether that description is fair we cannot know, although it is true that Thomas's writings contain a number of affectionate references to his father and none to his mother. We do not know much more about her, but we do know that she was proud of her boy, especially his authorship of *Common Sense.* Late in her life, Frances annually combined her piety and her pride in a July 4 fast celebrating her son's role in the American Revolution.[2]

Joseph Pain, Thomas's father, was an artisan, a maker of stays for corsets, which were ladies' undergarments designed to thin the waist and emphasize the curves of breasts and hips. He was the son of a

---

[1]The family spelling is *Pain,* but Thomas added the *e* when he published *Common Sense* in 1776 and retained it for the rest of his life.

[2]Francis Oldys [George Chalmers], *The Life of Thomas Pain* (London, 1791), 3.

farmer and neighbors described him as "a reputable citizen and though poor an honest man." Joseph Pain was also a Quaker. His marriage to an Anglican resulted in his expulsion from Meeting. Thereafter, Joseph was welcome at Quaker meetings for worship, but he was no longer a member. Indeed, it was not uncommon for expelled members to continue attending worship services, which Joseph did. Although Thomas was baptized and confirmed in the Church of England, his mother's religion, throughout his childhood he also attended Quaker meetings for worship with his father.[3]

The tug between the family's two religions contributed to Thomas Paine's skepticism and to his sense of himself as an outsider—an attender, but not a member of his father's religion, and a member, but not a true believer in his mother's church. He knew, firsthand, how harshly each religion judged the other and he judged them both. He saw the hypocrisies and imbibed the moral values of each. As a youth, Thomas Paine was neither irreligious nor antireligion, but as an adult he became skeptical of institutionalized Christianity.

The Quaker meetinghouse that Paine attended with his father held no more than fifty people, a small percentage of the town's two thousand souls. In all of England, the Society of Friends numbered no more than forty thousand of the kingdom's six to seven million people. And yet, by inclination and conviction, the Quakers stood proud and stubborn against the tide of popular beliefs. They denounced injustices that others failed to perceive. Surely Paine, infamous as an adult for the same stubborn righteousness, honed those qualities among these plain folk, for whom simplicity was a virtue and ostentation a vice. Like them, he was never surer he was right than when everyone else believed he was wrong. He relished challenging those above him in the cause of justice for those below. He demanded universal "equality" in *Common Sense,* when other revolutionaries claimed "liberty" only for the few. This stance was typical of the Quakers, who believed in the equality of all souls in the eyes of God long before others on either side of the Atlantic understood the social, political, and racial implications of this powerful testimony.[4]

The place where he lived was another formative influence on young Thomas Paine and thus on *Common Sense.* He grew up in a thatched

---

[3] Ibid., 3–4.
[4] William C. Braithwaite, *The Beginnings of Quakerism to 1660* (1912; 1955; Cambridge, England, 1981); Braithwaite, *The Second Period of Quakerism* (1919; 1961; Cambridge, England, 1979).

cottage in Thetford, England, which was located in 400 square miles of heath, a striking windswept landscape that was also home to some of England's rarest species of plants, insects, and birds. Contemporaries described the air as "bracing," imbued with the smell of Scotch pines, which harbored wild ducks at their base and stone curlews in their limbs. Indeed, the Pains' cottage was on the slope of a hill called the Wilderness, which evokes its marginal status on a frontier. Thomas Paine grew up on this margin. As a result, throughout his life he carried an appreciation of nature and a love of animal and plant life, which was surely a product of many days spent with his back to the town and his eyes on a landscape less constructed by humans.[5]

The earliest surviving writing of Thomas Paine's is an epitaph for a pet crow, which he wrote at the age of eight:

> *Here lies the body of John Crow,*
> *Who once was high but now is low;*
> *Ye brother Crows take warning all,*
> *For as you rise, so must you fall.*

Here we see Paine's attachment to a creature of the heath linked to his already militant sense of social justice. Already he was preaching in the high moral tone that is a hallmark of *Common Sense.* Already, after only one year in school, he wrote with clarity and force, in a language simple, accessible, and powerfully true to its earthy roots.[6]

The freedom that Paine found in nature as a boy was restricted in significant ways when he traveled from heath to town. For example, singing and playing musical instruments were illegal on Sundays in Thetford, as were ball games, cards, and skittles—a barroom gambling game played with a spinning top that randomly fells wooden pins. No music, fun, or games on the Sabbath was still the rule when Thomas Paine was growing up.[7]

Not every day was dull in Thetford, for it was the site of the spring, or Lenten, assizes, which swelled the population of the town for a week each year. These springtime court proceedings brought judge and barrister, prisoners and spectators, vendors and shoppers together in a raucous tradition. The spirit was solemn and celebratory

[5] John Keane, *Tom Paine: A Political Life* (Boston, 1995), 10.
[6] Ibid., 25.
[7] Ibid., 5.

at the same time. The streets, courtroom, tavern, and shops were noisy and full. Not everyone was there, though, to have a good time.

English justice was brutal in the eighteenth century. The Black Act of 1723 encompassed virtually all imaginable crimes, including challenges to public order and offenses against property and persons. By one count, this single piece of legislation identified between 200 and 250 offenses, all of them punishable by death. Even worse, the Black Act was so loosely worded that judges expanded greatly on the literal language of the law and the known intentions of its drafters. And the Black Act was just one, albeit the worst, of England's vicious criminal statutes.[8]

Thomas Paine and the prisoners tried at the Thetford assizes were born into a society that valued property above persons. His countrymen feared disorder most of all. They saw punishment as the most promising cure for poverty. Just as physicians of the day drained blood from patients to cure them of a wide range of diseases, so the judicial system sought to eliminate the poor—through death or banishment to the American colonies—as a solution to social ills. Neither bleeding nor retributive "justice" worked. Both killed more people than they saved.

The Wilderness where Thomas Paine grew up took its name not just from its soil, setting, and winds. It was also Thetford's execution site. The Wilderness gallows was kept busy throughout Paine's youth, ending the lives of those who hunted illegally because they were hungry, stole wood because they were cold, hurt others out of rage, or damaged property in a poor man's political statement against social injustice. The crowds that gathered to watch convicted criminals hang were so close to the Pains' cottage that they likely disturbed the baby's nap. Jailers herded convicts from the "cage," the jail located about one-quarter mile away, up a chalk ridge called Gallows Hill within clear sight of the cottage and earshot of Paine's crib.[9]

In the first spring of Thomas Paine's life, there were three executions. James Blade, aged forty-one, was a ship's carpenter who confessed to stealing money and goods valued at forty shillings from the King's Head Tavern in nearby Stanfield four years earlier. He

---

[8] E. P. Thompson, *Whigs and Hunters: The Origin of the Black Act* (New York, 1975); Douglas Hay et al., *Albion's Fatal Tree: Crime and Society in Eighteenth-Century England* (London, 1975); John Brewer and John Styles, eds., *An Ungovernable People: The English and Their Law in the Seventeenth and Eighteenth Centuries* (New Brunswick, N.J.: 1980).

[9] Keane, *Tom Paine*, 3.

also confessed to the crime of "keeping fairs." In other words, he threw parties at which people paid an entry fee to play such "disorderly" games as pricking the girdle, thimbles and ball, and a new one called black joke. The second execution was of William Wright, "a poor stupid Creature" from Suffolk County, who stole a bushel of wheat from a barn and robbed a woman on the highway by cutting off her pocket and stealing its contents—one guinea, six shillings, and six pence.[10]

John Painter, who was about thirty-five years old, was the third man executed that spring. He had a wife and children and kept and sold rabbits for a living. The court convicted him of purchasing a stolen horse and pilfering a parcel of tea. He vehemently denied the charges, claiming that the most unlawful thing that he ever did in his life was to poach rabbits from a nearby warren. It is possible that even if the court believed his denial of the charges on which he was brought to trial, his confession to stealing rabbits was more than enough to hang Painter under a common interpretation of the Black Act.[11]

Paine never mentioned whether he, like his neighbors and the visitors who flooded Thetford each spring, viewed the executions. As he grew older—ten, eleven, twelve—Paine could have watched the hangings of children younger than himself for stealing small amounts of food. Since he lived his first nineteen years in the shadow of Gallows Hill, it is likely that Paine shared in the horror and the thrill of the crowds who taunted the wretched prisoners and cheered the snap and swing of the rope. Did he, like other boys, throw stones at any of the scores of condemned men and women whose last steps carried them so close to where he took his first? When he was thirteen, Paine could have seen, heard, and smelled the execution of Amy Hutchinson, who was only four years older than him, for poisoning her husband. "Her face and hands," a newspaper reported, "were smeared with tar, and having a garment daubed with pitch, after a short prayer the executioner strangled her, and twenty minutes after the fire was kindled and burnt half an hour."[12]

The annual executions may have been Paine's first experience of state violence and a source of his highly attuned sensitivity to injustice. Executing a hungry child who took food, an unemployed father

---

[10]Keane, *Tom Paine*, 6; Ian Gilmour, *Riot, Risings and Revolution: Governance and Violence in Eighteenth Century England* (London, 1992); J. S. Cockburn, ed., *Crime in England 1550–1800* (London, 1977).

[11]Thompson, *Whigs and Hunters*; Keane, *Tom Paine*, 6.

[12]Moncure Daniel Conway, *The Life of Thomas Paine*, 2 vols. (New York, 1893), 1: 9.

who hunted illegally on a rich man's estate, or an impoverished mother for poaching firewood was the sort of abuse of power that riled Paine. The hangings may have emblazoned on his soul a passionate distrust of the authority exercised by government. On Sundays, when he attended Quaker meeting for worship with his father, Paine walked right past the prisoners awaiting their fate. The meetinghouse on Cage Lane was adjacent to the pillory, stocks, and "cage" or jail where the accused and the convicted were held. Meeting in silence, the boy and his fellow worshipers heard the wails of despondent souls, whose crimes paled in the Quakers' eyes before those of their executioners.[13]

The prisoners incarcerated next to the meetinghouse and the executions near Paine's home were not the only evidence around him that social justice was not embodied in the state. Even the poor who were not accused of theft, including those unable to work because of illness or injury, were routinely driven out of Thetford. Unmarried pregnant women were also bullied into leaving, lest their children become public burdens. It was, in effect, a crime just to be poor in eighteenth-century England and the punishments included cruelty, whippings, transportation to the American colonies, and the gallows. British society blamed the destitute for their condition and treated them as if hunger and homelessness were just wages for their sins. At that time, about half of England's population was unable to feed itself for at least part of each year. Seasonal labor resulted in seasonal hunger and crime, and a vicious response in Thetford and elsewhere in the nation of Paine's birth.[14]

The gap between poor and rich was clear to Paine and others in Thetford. All the town's residents lived subject to the whims of Euston Hall, the vast estate of the Duke of Grafton, which encompassed more than forty square miles. The power that its occupants brandished was equally vast. Thetford was a "rotten borough," which meant that the town's elected members of Parliament were hand-picked by a few powerful men. Purchasing votes, distributing favors, and threatening those whom they could not buy, the Dukes of Grafton controlled the political process in Thetford throughout the eighteenth century. The last contested election of the century was in 1733, four years before Thomas Paine's birth. There were only thirty voters in the town and

---

[13] Ibid., 10.
[14] Thompson, *Whigs and Hunters*; Hay, *Albion's Fatal Tree*; Peter Linebaugh, *The London Hanged: Crime and Civil Society in the Eighteenth Century* (New York, 1992).

they bowed to the Duke of Grafton's will on matters of local and national politics.[15]

This is the sort of corruption that Paine found at the very heart of the British Constitution. While Americans were prone to worship the British constitutional tradition, Paine's first-hand experiences led him to declare in *Common Sense* that English politics was morally dead. Where Americans had viewed the British scene from a great distance and through the lenses of common-law theorists such as Edward Coke and William Blackstone, Paine offered a cynical indictment of the British pretense to justice based, at least in part, on his witnessing of brutality, injustice, and corruption in Thetford.

GROWING UP

George Chalmers, Paine's first biographer, described him as "a sharp boy, of unsettled application." His parents sent him to the local grammar school, which cost more than they could afford and thus represented a powerful commitment to their son's education, and perhaps ambitions for him that reached beyond their status. "My parents were not able to give me a shilling," Paine later recalled, "beyond what they gave me in education; and to do this they distressed themselves." As a Quaker, Paine's father was more concerned with moral education than book-learning, but wanted his son to receive his full share of "useful" knowledge as well. "His tuition was directed," according to the eighteenth-century biographer, "to what is useful, more than to what is ornamental; to reading, writing, and cyphering, which are so commodious to tradesmen, rather than to classical knowledge, which is so decorous in gentlemen."[16]

At the age of twelve, Thomas left school to serve the standard seven-year apprenticeship in his father's corsetmaker's trade. Corset stays were made of whalebone, which was cut, shaped, and stitched into woolen cloth that was lined with linen. These were tedious tasks, requiring patience, concentration, and skill. In the end, the product was subject to the whims of fashion and, to Thomas Paine's apparent misfortune, the fashion for corsets was entering a period of comparative decline just as he was serving the last years of his apprenticeship.[17]

---

[15]Keane, *Tom Paine,* 9–15.
[16]Oldys, *Life of Thomas Pain,* 4; Conway, *Life of Thomas Paine,* 11–12.
[17]Keane, *Tom Paine,* 29–31.

With dim economic prospects, Paine ran off looking for adventure and enlisted on a privateer, a ship called the *Terrible*. A privateer was one of many licensed commercial ventures that took advantage of war to attack the ships of enemy nations for their plunder. These sanctioned pirates lived a dangerous life; about half of them ended up dead, seriously injured, or as prisoners of war. Fortunately for Thomas, Joseph Pain arrived in time to convince his son not to sail on the *Terrible;* only seventeen of the approximately 170 men on board survived the voyage.[18]

Within a month, though, the impetuous Thomas Paine did set sail on the *King of Prussia,* a voyage that he not only survived but from which he profited greatly. Upon his return to London in 1757, Paine gave up the privateer's life. Restless, unsuccessful, and ill-tempered according to later accounts, he moved from London to Dover (1758) and then to Sandwich (1759). There may have been a romance in Dover, from which Paine fled owing the girl's father ten pounds that he never repaid. In Sandwich, if not before, Paine tried his hand at preaching—possibly as an "Independent" or Congregationalist, more likely as a Methodist—and apparently had a small following. He also tried yet again to set up a staymaking shop, but that failed.[19]

In Sandwich, Paine met Mary Lambert, a waiting maid who was the daughter of a local excise tax collector, and who, according to local tradition, was "a pretty girl of modest behavior." They married in the town's Anglican church on September 27, 1759, when Thomas was twenty-two and Mary a year younger. According to Paine's first biographer, "the women of Sandwich, to this hour, express their surprise, *that so fine a girl should have married so old a fellow.*" The biographer took this to mean that Paine "always appeared to female eyes a dozen years older than he was, owing to the hardness of his features, or to the scars of disease." Possibly smallpox marked Paine's face; perhaps hard living already showed on his countenance. In any event, Paine apparently expected a dowry with his new wife and was greatly disappointed when one did not materialize.[20]

Whether it was financial disappointment, drinking, sexual dysfunction, or just his temperament, we cannot know, but Paine abused his wife from a very early stage in their marriage. "Two months had hardly elapsed," George Chalmers heard, "when [Paine's] ill usage of his wife

---

[18] Ibid., 31–35.
[19] Oldys, *Life of Thomas Pain,* 5; Keane, *Tom Paine,* 36–52.
[20] Oldys, *Life of Thomas Pain,* 5.

became apparent to the whole town, and excited the indignation of some, with the pity of others." Since spousal abuse was very common, very rarely prosecuted, and largely uncommented upon during the eighteenth century, there must have been striking qualities to this case. Perhaps it was the loudness of tirades that called attention to Paine's behavior or physical evidence of Paine's brutality on Mary's body and face. Whatever the cause, whatever the evidence, Paine was an infamous wife-beater in an age when such infamy was not easily achieved.[21]

Thomas and Mary Paine lived in poverty for about twelve months in Sandwich before Paine rented a house and purchased furniture for it on credit. Apparently Paine planned to defraud his landlord and creditor from the outset, because soon after the move to nicer accommodations, he and his wife absconded to Margate where Paine sold the furniture at auction and pocketed the cash. Shortly thereafter, Mary died in childbirth, as did the child she bore. Rumors circulated that Paine's abuse resulted in a premature delivery and accounted for his wife's death. We cannot know, however, whether such rumors are true.[22]

EXCISE MAN

Within two years of Mary's death, Paine undertook a new career as an excise tax collector. In 1762, at the age of twenty-five, he began gauging stills for the purpose of taxing liquor in Grantham. Next he was employed to catch smugglers at Alford. In August 1765, Paine was dismissed from this job under circumstances that are not entirely clear; it may have been, unfairly, for calling attention to a supervisor's corruption. About one year later, in July 1766, Paine was reinstated after apologizing for official misconduct. Between collecting excise taxes, he also taught reading and writing to artisans' children, ran a tobacco shop, and did some itinerant Methodist preaching in Lewes beginning in March 1768. In 1774, Paine lost his excise collector's job permanently for writing a pamphlet called *The Case of the Officers of Excise* (1772), which represented to Parliament the tax collectors' case for increased wages. He was formally charged with being absent from his duties without permission, which was technically true since he distributed pamphlets in London when his posting was to Lewes, in Sussex. It is also possible that Paine was selling smuggled tobacco in

---

[21]Ibid.
[22]Keane, *Tom Paine,* 50–51; Oldys, *Life of Thomas Pain,* 6–7.

his shop, and that such flouting of the laws he was supposed to enforce was a contributing factor in his dismissal.[23]

Paine remarried in 1771, at the age of thirty-four. His new wife, Elizabeth Ollive, was eleven years younger than Paine and the daughter of the widow whose tobacco shop he managed in Lewes to supplement his tax collector's salary. In 1774, when Paine lost his excise collector's job and the tobacco shop was faring poorly, his second marriage ended in a legal separation. George Chalmers inquired about the second marriage and local people recounted stories much like those he had heard about the first. "What had been seen at Sandwich of his conjugal tyranny," the biographer reported, "was ere long observed at Lewes. Such was the meekness of his wife that she suffered patiently: but as his embarrassments did not mollify a temper, which is from nature harsh; as his subordination to others did not soften his treatment of inferiors, from neglect of his wife, he proceeded to contumely; from contumely he went on to cruelty; when being no longer able to support his repeated beatings, she complained to her friends."[24]

With creditors closing in on him, and rumors that he had been unable to consummate his marriage during its three-year duration dogging his heels, Paine signed the separation agreement with his wife and left one last time for London. Later in life, Paine responded to a friend's inquiry about the separation, that "it is nobody's business but my own; I had a cause for it but will name it to no one." Another friend remarked, though, that "Thomas Paine always spoke tenderly and respectfully of his wife; and sent her several times pecuniary aid, without her knowing even whence it came."[25]

Paine never married again and there is no evidence of any kind that ever linked him to another woman. He was thereafter often described as having a fiery temper. His drinking became legendary. And remarks on his appearance and body odor, in an age far more odiferous than ours, suggest that whether the oral traditions are all true in every detail, they represent fairly the ornery temperament of the man they describe. Perhaps Paine suffered from depression, but he clearly had a tendency to tell people off and become isolated from others. We can be sure, though, that 1774 was one of the lowest, if not the most disheartening, times of Thomas Paine's life.[26]

[23] Keane, *Tom Paine,* 52–79; Oldys, *Life of Thomas Pain,* 7.
[24] Oldys, *Life of Thomas Pain,* 10–11.
[25] Conway, *Life of Thomas Paine,* 31, 36.
[26] Oldys, *Life of Thomas Pain,* 8.

PASSAGES

At this time, if not before, Paine began contemplating a new start in England's American colonies. He was bankrupt, had few personal connections in England, and was a failure in every respect that mattered to him. Just as so many other immigrants, Paine hoped that his prospects would brighten, that he could start his life over, and that America would recognize his talents in ways that his homeland did not. "I happened," Paine wrote later in life, "when a schoolboy to pick up a pleasing natural history of Virginia, and my inclination from that day of seeing the western side of the Atlantic never left me." Now, Paine hoped to fulfill that boyhood dream and put the failures of the first thirty-seven years of his life literally behind him as he set sail for the New World and a new life.[27]

In London, Paine had met Benjamin Franklin through a mutual friend. Franklin was impressed by conversations he had with Paine and Paine was undoubtedly encouraged by Franklin's enthusiasm for Philadelphia. Franklin encouraged Paine to emigrate from London and wrote a letter of introduction to ease the Englishman's entry into Philadelphia society. "The bearer, Mr. Thomas Paine," Franklin wrote to his son-in-law, "is very well recommended to me, as an ingenious, worthy young man. He goes to Pennsylvania with a view of settling there."[28]

Paine booked first-class passage on the *London Packet,* using the money from his financial settlement with his wife. The ship left London during the autumn of 1774 and arrived in Philadelphia some time between December 7 and 12. It was a rough eight-week passage. Paine suffered brutally from seasickness and then, along with almost all of the ship's 120 passengers, he contracted typhus. The "putrid fever," as he called it, was generally contracted from lice and brought on bad headaches, a flushed and swollen face, sleeplessness, high fever, violent delirium, diarrhea, and a general listlessness. By the time the ship landed, the survivors were very weak and in need of several weeks' rest to recover. Before the end of the month, though, Paine was writing and shortly began looking for work.[29]

Franklin and Paine both thought that he would find his first job as a tutor or schoolteacher, one of the several occupations that he had in

[27] Conway, *Life of Thomas Paine,* 12.
[28] Benjamin Franklin to Richard Bache, September 30, 1774, *Papers of Benjamin Franklin,* 21 (1978), 325–26.
[29] Frank Smith, "New Light on Thomas Paine's First Year in America, 1775," *American Literature,* 1 (1929–30): 348–49; Keane, *Tom Paine,* 83–84.

England. But as Paine explained to Franklin, he quickly found work as a writer and editor, which was a career that appealed to him even more: "a Printer and Bookseller here, a Man of Reputation, and Property (Robt. Aitken) has lately attempted a Magazine, but having little or no turn that Way himself has applied to me for assistance. He had not above 600 Subscribers when I first assisted him. We have now upwrds of 1500, and daily encreasing."[30]

SLAVERY

Even before Paine got his editor's job, he began writing. Among his first essays was "African Slavery in America," which was published in a new journal called *The Pennsylvania Magazine* in early March. (See Document 1.) This piece gave Americans their first exposure to Paine's unique stylistic mix of passion and directness, and his willingness to take an unpopular stand.

> To AMERICANS.
> THAT some desperate wretches should be willing to steal and enslave men by violence and murder for gain, is rather lamentable than strange. But that many civilized, nay, christianized people should approve, and be concerned in the savage practice, is surprising; and still persist, though it has been so often proved contrary to the light of nature, to every principle of Justice and Humanity, and even good policy, by a succession of eminent men, and several late publications.[31] (p. 58)

In the first paragraph of the essay we see the strong words "wretches" and "savage," with which, along with his punctuated use of uppercase letters, Paine intended to stun readers. The phrase "light of nature" conjoins the Quaker and naturalist influences of his youth.

---

[30]Thomas Paine to Benjamin Franklin, 4 Mar. 1775, ibid., 515–16.

[31]Thomas Paine, "African Slavery in America," *Pennsylvania Journal,* 8 Mar. 1775, in Moncure Conway, ed., *Writings of Thomas Paine,* I, 4. Paine's authorship of this essay has recently been questioned by James V. Lynch, "The Limits of Revolutionary Radicalism: Tom Paine and Slavery," *Pennsylvania Magazine of History and Biography,* 123 (1999): 177–99. The author's principal reason for questioning Paine's authorship is that the attribution by Dr. Benjamin Rush was made when Rush was an old man in an account that confused the chronology of Paine's arrival in America and Rush's first meeting with him. Lynch also contends that the style of the essay is significantly different from Paine's other writings. In doing this, Lynch ignores Frank Smith's careful, and fully convincing, discussion of Rush's attribution and the essay's stylistic similarities to other writings by Paine in "New Light on Thomas Paine's First Year in America, 1775." Smith's remains the standard, and most reliable, study of Paine's 1775 writings and Lynch's neglect even to cite Smith's article is puzzling, especially in light of his use of another essay by Lynch to support other claims.

W. Ralph, *Negroes Just Landed from a Slave Ship*. Engraving, 1808.
Print Collection, Miriam and Ira D. Wallach Division of Art, Prints and Photographs,
The New York Public Library, Astor, Lennox and Tilden Foundations.

The appeal to nature continues throughout the short essay. Paine describes slaves as *"an unnatural commodity!,"* who were treated like "wild beasts." The contrast between what is "natural," and therefore good, and "unnatural," and therefore evil, runs through the essay and also appears in *Common Sense*. Paine cast "unnatural" wars and commodities against the redemptive qualities of "natural, perfect" rights, "natural" ties, and the "natural dictates of conscience." Likewise, Paine found "natural satisfaction" superior to unnatural desires and felt natural abhorrence for unnatural acts.

As we will see again in *Common Sense*, Paine pitted his reading of the Bible against those who justified their "unnatural" behavior with biblical passages that he believed they either misunderstood or quoted out of context. He was eager to match such opponents quotation for quotation in a battle for the morally higher ground. "Most shocking of all," Paine argues, "is alledging the Sacred Scriptures to favour this wicked practice" of slavery. "One would have thought none but infidel cavillers would endeavour to make them appear contrary to the plain dictates of natural light, and Conscience, in a matter of common Justice and Humanity; which they cannot be."[32]

---

[32] Ibid., 5–6.

Brilliantly, Paine tried to shake readers out of their complacent acceptance of slavery with provocative rhetorical questions and a bold, challenging reply.

> Is the barbarous enslaving our inoffensive neighbours, and treating them like wild beasts subdued by force, reconcilable with all these *Divine precepts?* Is this doing to them as we would desire they should do to us? If they could carry off and enslave some thousands of us, would we think it just?—One would almost wish they could for once; it might convince more than Reason, or the Bible.[33] (See Document 1.)

In the end, Paine intended to leave no safe ground for a Christian implicated in the institution of slavery, no rationalization, no biblical authority, nowhere to hide from his conscience, his God, and the social evil around him. Paine meant to make his readers uncomfortable, unable to live in peace with their acceptance of the status quo.

Paine found justifications for slavery based in history and law just as defective as those based on the Bible. Both natural right and justice dictated that Christians free their slaves and rid society of its evil taint.

> As much in vain, perhaps, will they search ancient history for examples of the modern Slave-Trade. Too many nations enslaved the prisoners they took in war. But to go to nations with whom there is no war, who have no way provoked, without farther design of conquest, purely to catch inoffensive people, like wild beasts, for slaves, is an hight of outrage against Humanity and Justice, that seems left by Heathen nations to be practised by pretended Christians. How shameful are all attempts to colour and excuse it![34] (See Document 1.)

In his brief time in America, Paine had already learned that some people rationalized slavery as a necessary evil, justified by the impracticality of releasing the slaves. Americans feared what would happen once the slaves were set free. They foresaw increased crime and reprisals for ill treatment, violence, and social unrest. And what about compensation, they asked, for masters who lost the value of their slave property through emancipation? Let legislatures decide on the amounts and means for compensating masters, Paine reasoned, in effect begging the point. As for the slaves:

> Perhaps they might sometime form useful barrier settlements on the frontiers. Thus they may become interested in the public welfare, and

[33] Ibid., 6.
[34] Ibid., 6–7.

assist in promoting it; instead of being dangerous, as now they are, should any enemy promise them a better condition.[35] (See Document 1.)

Finally, Paine told his readers, Pennsylvanians and other Americans owed slaves at least the rudiments of education, both as compensation for what they suffered in slavery and as a legacy to the generations to follow. It was the right thing to do, the obvious thing to do, and a matter of both reason and conscience that the problem be addressed immediately. It was the sentiment of "JUSTICE AND HUMANITY," as Paine signed himself, that readers must act. Some Pennsylvanians did act, and quickly. About five weeks after Paine's essay on slavery appeared, on April 14, 1775, "The Society for the Relief of Free Negroes, unlawfully held in bondage" was formed.[36]

Paine's next piece of antislavery writing, "A Serious Thought," appeared in the fall of 1775. In this essay, Paine extended his reach to connect his antislavery arguments to the cause of American independence from Great Britain.

> When I reflect on the horrid cruelties exercised by Britain in the East Indies...I firmly believe that the Almighty, in compassion to mankind, will curtail the power of Britain.... And when to these and many other melancholy reflections I add this sad remark, that ever since the discovery of America she hath employed herself in the most horrid of all traffics, that of human flesh, unknown to the most savage nations, hath yearly (without provocation and in cold blood) ravaged the hapless shores of Africa, robbing it of its unoffending inhabitants to cultivate her stolen dominions in the West—When I reflect on these, I hesitate not for a moment to believe that the Almighty will finally separate America from Britain. Call it Independence or what you will, if it is the cause of God and humanity it will go on. (See Document 2.)

Carrying the logic of his historical projection one huge step further than Thomas Jefferson would six months later in his draft of the Declaration of Independence, Paine imagined past the Revolution to independence, when the burden of righting this great wrong would fall decisively on Americans.

> And when the Almighty shall have blest us, and made us a people *dependent only upon Him,* then may our first gratitude be shown by an act of continental legislation, which shall put a stop to the importation

---

[35] Ibid., 8.
[36] Gary B. Nash and Jean R. Soderlund, *Freedom by Degrees: Emancipation in Pennsylvania and Its Aftermath* (New York, 1991), 79, 101, 124.

of Negroes for sale, soften the hard fate of those already here, and in time procure their freedom.[37] (See Document 2.)

BRITISH ARMY

Two other essays that Paine wrote in 1775 address the "enslavement" of colonists by the British military. Since they appeared in the *Pennsylvania Journal* during the same year as "African Slavery in America" and "A Serious Thought," the connection between the colonists' "slavery" and the freedom that Paine advocated for their slaves was both ironic and intriguing. It is also significant that Paine considered "defensive war" against the British a viable option at least six months before the publication of *Common Sense*.

The first of these essays was an imagined dialogue between General James Wolfe, the martyred hero of Great Britain's assault on Quebec during the Seven Years' War (1754–1763), and General Thomas Gage, the British commander of forces stationed in Boston in 1775. (See Document 3.) In this conversation, Wolfe's ghost explained that he was sent by a delegation of British military heroes to deliver a message.

> You are come upon a business unworthy a British soldier, and a freeman. You have come here to deprive your fellow subjects of their liberty.

When Gage responded that he was simply following the orders of his king, as a good soldier should, the ghost reprimanded him for forgetting that his duty was to the king *and* his "COUNTRY."

> The American colonies are entitled to all the privileges of British subjects. Equality of liberty is the glory of every Briton. He does not forfeit it by crossing the Ocean. He carries it with him into the most distant parts of the world, because he carries with him the immutable laws of nature. A Briton or an American ceases to be a British subject when he ceases to be governed by rulers chosen or approved of by himself. This is the essence of liberty and of the British constitution.[38] (See Document 3.)

[37]Thomas Paine, "A Serious Thought," *Pennsylvania Journal,* 18 Oct. 1775, in Moncure Daniel Conway, ed., *The Writings of Thomas Paine,* 2 vols. (New York, 1894–1896; New York, 1967), 1: 65–66; Pauline Maier, *American Scripture: Making the Declaration of Independence* (New York, 1997), App. C, 239; Joseph Ellis, *American Sphinx: The Character of Thomas Jefferson* (New York, 1997), 7, 18, 51–52.

[38]Thomas Paine, "A Dialogue between General Wolfe and General Gage in a Wood Near Boston," *Pennsylvania Journal,* 4 Jan. 1775, in Conway, ed., *Writings of Thomas Paine,* 1: 11.

George Townshend, *General James Wolfe* (1727–1759).
With permission of the McCord Museum of Canadian History,
Montreal.

Paine's dialogue thus gave Wolfe's ghost some very American thoughts.
He endorsed the colonists' dissent from British notions of "virtual"
representation and their linking of direct election of representatives,
local administration of government, and the "liberty" that they
asserted as English subjects. Essentially, Americans believed in direct
representation by delegates for whom they voted, who lived in their
neighborhood, and who represented their interests in legislative bodies. Alternatively, the British model endorsed the notion that every
Member of Parliament represented the interests of the whole Empire,
and that the link between residence and local interests was contrary
to good governance.

John Singleton Copley, *General Thomas Gage,* c. 1769. Gage
(1719 or 1720–1787) was the commander in chief of the
British army in North America from 1763 to 1775.
William L. Clements Library, University of Michigan.

General Wolfe's ghost justified American resistance to the Massachusetts Government Reorganization Act and the Quebec Act, two of
the hated "Intolerable Acts" imposed on the colonies as punishment
for the Boston Tea Party. The ghost also reflected the colonists'
Protestant bigotry against French "popery" and "despotism," which
they contrasted with their traditional freedom. The ghost saw Britain's
administrative and military responses to American resistance in the
same light that he viewed seventeenth-century assaults on the rights
of Englishmen, and encouraged Gage to act with independence and
courage.

The edicts of the British parliament (for they want the sanction of British laws) which relate to the province of Massachusetts Bay are big with destruction to the whole British empire. I come therefore in the name of... an illustrious band of English heroes to whom the glory of Old England is still dear to beg you to have no hand in the execution of them. You did not give up your privileges as a citizen when you put on your sword. British soldiers are not machines, to be animated only with the voice of a Minister of State. They disdain those ideas of submission which preclude them from the liberty of thinking for themselves, and degrade them to an equality with a war horse, or an elephant.[39] (See Document 3.)

Five months later, Paine published "Thoughts on Defensive War," an essay that engaged both the British, who were not taking his advice to abandon their occupation of Boston, and the Quakers, whom he already saw in the Pennsylvania context as threats to a war in defense of liberty. He found Quaker pacifism, the most literal expression of their testimony for peace, impractical in a world without angels and miracles. Paine wrote:

> I am thus far a Quaker, that I would gladly agree with all the world to lay aside the use of arms, and settle matters by negotiation; but unless the whole will, the matter ends, and I take up my musket and thank heaven he has put it in my power.[40] (See Document 4.)

Here Paine anticipated his open letter "To the Representatives of the Religious Society of Friends," which appeared as a postscript to the second and subsequent editions of *Common Sense.* His letter would expand on the same antipacifist themes that we see in "Thoughts on Defensive War," and the same impatience with Quakers, who spoke with less authority than they claimed on the Bible, politics, and the beliefs of the Society of Friends. In both pieces, Paine alluded to his Quaker past and claimed better authority to speak for the Society of Friends than those American Quakers who endorsed a pacifist path. This fluid movement from authoritative insider to clear-sighted outsider, when it suited his argument, was a device that permeated *Common Sense* as well as these earlier writings.

The high moral tone of "Thoughts on Defensive War" was also distinctively Paine's. "Whoever considers the unprincipled enemy we have to cope with," wrote Paine, "will not hesitate to declare that nothing but

---

[39] Conway, ed., *Writings of Thomas Paine,* 1: 12.

[40] Thomas Paine, "Thoughts on Defensive War," *Pennsylvania Journal,* July 1775, in Conway, ed., *Writings of Thomas Paine,* 1: 55.

Amos Doolittle, *Battle of Lexington,* Massachusetts, 1775, depicts the opening shots of the Revolution. It shows the British as aggressors and the militia as attempting to flee the field without resistance. In fact, the first shots fired by the British soldiers were not ordered by their officers and were apparently a response to a shot fired by a colonial bystander.
The Granger Collection, New York.

arms or miracles can reduce them to reason and moderation. They have lost sight of the limits of humanity."[41] The British were thieves, literally "highwaymen," who stole American rights and wealth as well. They robbed and insulted Americans, whom they imagined incapable of self-defense.

> ...the position laid down by Lord Sandwich is a clear demonstration of the justice of defensive arms. The Americans, quoth this Quixote of modern days, *will not fight;* therefore we will. His Lordship's plan when analized amounts to this. These people are either too superstitiously religious, or too cowardly for arms; they either *cannot* or *dare not* defend; their property is open to any one who has the courage to attack

[41] Ibid.

them. Send but your troops and the prize is ours. Kill a few and take the whole.[42] (See Document 4.)

The choice before Americans, Paine reasoned, was simple: either stand up to the "invader," the "plunderer," the "ruffian" or lose everything.

It was already late in the day for a military response, reasoned Paine in July 1775. The quicker and more forceful the defense, the less blood would be spilled in the end. Each passing day emboldened the aggressor, and convinced the British that Americans lacked the courage to defend their liberties.

> The lives of hundreds of both countries had been preserved had America been in arms a year ago. Our enemies have mistaken our peace for cowardice, and supposing us unarmed have begun the attack.[43] (See Document 4.)

Paine signed himself "A Lover of Peace," even as he boldly defined Great Britain as America's enemy and advocated the taking up of arms against the British only eight months after he emigrated from what he now termed the "enemy's" shores. This alienation from his homeland and the speed of Paine's transition from Briton to American is stunning. His fast read and sure grasp of the American perspective was brilliant. As a social outsider and a failure in business and marriage in Britain, Paine's alienation from his homeland preceded his Atlantic crossing. This alienated British perspective took quick and sure root in colonial soil, where Americans shared Paine's feelings of marginality but were just a bit slower and less confident about asserting their distinctiveness as a virtue.

MARRIAGE

One of Paine's 1775 essays reflects on his private failures back in England and thus connects the public and private alienation that led him to blame the English for both his own and his fellow Americans' problems. Aptly entitled "Reflections on Unhappy Marriages," the essay lays out in general terms some of Paine's own marital issues. Lust and a passion for beauty, Paine cautions, are poor rationales for marriage. Initial attraction to a pretty face is no guarantee of connubial bliss. Indeed, acting on physical appeal is what undoes

---

[42] Ibid.
[43] Ibid., 57–58.

Lewis Miller, *Henry Sheffer and His Wife,* sketch of a quarreling couple, York, Pennsylvania, c. 1806.
The York County Heritage Trust, Pennsylvania. Detail. Artist Lewis Miller (1796–1882).

the young, the rash and amorous, whose hearts are ever glowing with desire, whose eyes are ever roaming after beauty; these doat [dote] on the first amiable image that chance throws in their way, and when the flame is once kindled would risk eternity itself to appease it.[44] (See Document 5.)

Then, after the wedding, when their eyes have feasted to boredom and their lusts are quenched, the couple realizes the mistake. Like Adam and Eve,

their first parents, they no sooner taste the tempting fruit, but their eyes are opened; the folly of their intemperance becomes visible; shame succeeds first and then repentance; but sorrow for themselves soon returns to anger with the innocent cause of their unhappiness. Hence flow bitter reproaches, and keen invectives, which end in mutual hatred and contempt. (See Document 5.)

Is this how Paine explained his violence—the cuts and the bruises that his neighbors said he inflicted on both of his wives? Does this essay reflect his personal "repentance"—a fascinating choice of words, which could express guilt, sorrow, and an attempt to forgive himself? Although

---

[44]Thomas Paine, "Reflections on Unhappy Marriages," *Pennsylvania Magazine,* June, 1775, in Conway, ed., *Writings of Thomas Paine,* 1: 51.

we cannot know for sure whether Paine consciously wrote about his own experiences, his words provide evidence to support informed speculation about how he dealt, at least subconsciously and perhaps consciously, with the trauma that he had caused his wives.[45]

Paine believed that this unfortunate method of spousal selection, in which the passions rule over rational choice, was endemic to the young, but not universal. He judged even more harshly those from the upper classes whose marital choices represented a rational calculation of economic gain. Such men, Paine declared, "hunt out a wife as they go to Smithfield for a horse; and inter-marry fortunes, not minds, or even bodies." According to Paine, the expectations of brides and grooms who enter matrimony as a business transaction are much lower than those of the passionate young lovers. Such "insipid" partners "are exactly as fond the twentieth year of matrimony, as the first." His observations on the upper classes were not, Paine pointed out, an endorsement of passionless marriage.

> Mere absence of pain will undoubtedly constitute ease; and, without ease, there can be no happiness: Ease, however, is but the medium, through which happiness is tasted, and but passively receives what the last actually bestows; if therefore the rash who marry inconsiderately, perish in the storms raised by their own passions, these slumber away their days in a sluggish calm, and rather dream they live, than experience it by a series of actual sensible enjoyments.[46] (See Document 5.)

Having savaged both marriages based on passion and on property, having predicted violence for one and declared the other the moral equivalent of prostitution, there were other places that Paine might have traveled in this essay. He could have visited the sort of spiritual bonds that others, such as the American theologian and minister Jonathan Edwards, described as the heart and soul of a good marriage.[47] He could have endorsed a form of courtly love, of the kind celebrated by William Shakespeare.

Since Paine believed that passion rules human choices, since he found spirituality and self-sacrifice uncommon, and since it seems that Paine quite possibly never knew romantic love, he headed instead in a direction inspired by an alternative vision of the American wilderness.

---

[45] Ibid.

[46] Ibid., 52.

[47] Jonathan Edwards, "Sarah Pierpont" (1723), in Giles Gunn, ed., *Early American Writing* (New York, 1994), 311–12.

To be sure, the model was Paine's, but he put the words in the mouth of an anonymous "American savage," a favorite device of writers on both sides of the Atlantic at that time. The symbol of "savage" wisdom both ridiculed "civilization" and drew on the "natural" imagery so central to Paine's thought. Paine's "savage" ridiculed Christian morality and declared more "natural" those unions based in mutual affections rather than legally and religiously sanctioned marriages.

> Whereas in ours, which have no other ceremony than mutual affection, and last no longer than they bestow mutual pleasures, we make it our business to oblige the heart we are afraid to lose; and being at liberty to separate, seldom or never feel the inclination. But if any should be found so wretched among us, as to hate where the only commerce ought to be love, we instantly dissolve the band: God made us all in pairs; each has his mate somewhere or other; and it is our duty to find each other out, since no creature was ever intended to be miserable.[48] (See Document 5.)

In this passage Paine revealed much of his inner self. It was a romantic, anti-institutional, spiritual, and alienated self. It was a man alone, who still dreamed that there was someone for him, someone who would be neither the cause nor the victim of pain. It was a man who believed that most of us, just like him, are "savages" at heart. This was not, in Paine's reasoning, a denunciation of human nature; indeed, Paine celebrated passion well spent. It does help explain, though, why Paine as a writer would aim for the heart over the head. He knew what led people to act. Sure, they had rationalizations based on morals, ideals, principles, and rules, but he knew better and would prove it when he wrote *Common Sense*.

It was Paine's genius to claim life on the periphery as a virtue and to see the metropolitan culture as inferior, morally bankrupt, and a vice. Such a vision suited Paine's life, his American experience, and the Revolutionary cause. The timing was as critical as the method and the message. Nothing that Paine published in 1775 set Philadelphia on fire, but as 1776 approached and his first year as an American came to an end, Paine again sharpened his pen, dipped it in ink, and wrote from the gut. The result was the lightning bolt called *Common Sense,* which electrified the political scene in Philadelphia and elsewhere as well.

---

[48] Conway, ed., *Writings of Thomas Paine,* 1: 53–54.

COMMON SENSE

Common Sense was "a masterly, irresistible performance," Charles Lee wrote to his fellow Virginian George Washington. It convinced Lee that independence from the British Empire was a necessity. "How is *Common Sense* rellish'd among you," Samuel Cooper asked Benjamin Franklin in a letter from New York; "it is eagerly read and greatly admired here." Neither Lee nor Cooper knew that Thomas Paine was the author. When the pamphlet appeared for sale on January 10, 1776, its authorship was anonymous and most guessed wrongly that it was the work of an American. Some believed that the writer was John Adams. Others reasoned that it must be a Philadelphian. Many years later, Thomas Jefferson complimented *Common Sense* by pointing out how well Thomas Paine's writing style compared with Benjamin Franklin's. "No writer has exceeded Paine in ease and familiarity of style," Jefferson wrote, "in perspicuity of expression, happiness of elucidation, and in simple and unassuming language. In this he may be compared with Dr. Franklin; and indeed his *Common Sense* was, for awhile, believed to have been written by Dr. Franklin."[49]

Paine apparently began work on the pamphlet during August and September 1775, assembling notes, gathering thoughts, and capturing compelling phrases. All that he had experienced in England was background; all that he wrote in 1775 was preparation. When he completed a section, Paine took it to the home of his friend, the Philadelphia physician Benjamin Rush. There, Paine read his words aloud, trusting his own ear and that of his friend for the pamphlet's pitch. This method of honing passages through oral readings vividly portrayed Paine's intent. He meant the words to ring in people's ears, to inspire them collectively by dramatic readings, to make revolution a communal experience.[50]

Paine worked and reworked the pamphlet during the fall. In early December, he completed a draft. Paine initially titled the pamphlet *Plain Truth.* Rush suggested *Common Sense.* David Rittenhouse, the

---

[49]Charles Lee to George Washington, *Lee Papers,* 1: 259–60; Samuel Cooper to Benjamin Franklin, 21 Mar. 1776, William B. Willcox, ed., *The Papers of Benjamin Franklin* (New Haven, 1982), 22: 388; Thomas Jefferson to Francis Eppes, 19 Jan. 1821, Merrill D. Peterson, ed., *Thomas Jefferson: Writings* (New York, 1984), 1451.

[50]Keane, *Tom Paine,* 106–7.

COMMON SENSE;

ADDRESSED TO THE

INHABITANTS

OF

A M E R I C A,

On the following interesting

SUBJECTS.

I. Of the Origin and Design of Government in general, with concise Remarks on the English Constitution.

II. Of Monarchy and Hereditary Succession.

III. Thoughts on the present State of American Affairs.

IV. Of the present Ability of America, with some miscellaneous Reflections.

A NEW EDITION, with several Additions in the Body of the Work. To which is added an APPENDIX ; together with an Address to the People called QUAKERS.

N. B. The New Addition here given increases the Work upwards of one Third.

Man knows no Master save creating HEAVEN,
Or those whom Choice and common Good ordain.
THOMSON.

PHILADELPHIA PRINTED.

And SOLD by W. and T. BRADFORD.

Common Sense, title page from second, expanded, edition printed by William Bradford and published on February 14, 1776.
The Library Company of Philadelphia.

astronomer famous for his observations of the transit of Venus in 1768, read it for Paine and gave him advice. Benjamin Franklin and Samuel Adams also helped Paine tinker with his text. Franklin, the greatest American prose writer of his day, knew words. Samuel Adams, the fiery Boston radical, was a master propagandist. Rush and Rittenhouse were men of science, logic, and more cautious temperament. All helped. Fortunately, though, the pamphlet was not the product of a committee. It was pure Paine.[51]

Publication and Circulation

Paine never said why he published the pamphlet anonymously, but it made sense to fear prosecution for treason should his identity become known. Benjamin Rush had warned him that "there were two words which he should avoid by every means as necessary to his own safety and that of the public—*independence* and *republicanism*." Paine ignored this advice, but did leave off his name. It was certainly not for lack of pride in authorship, because it was at this time that he added an *e* to his family's spelling of "Pain." Although he never explained this new identity, the timing speaks volumes to the significance of *Common Sense* in his life. This was a transforming event for the author as well as the American readers who marched off to war with copies in their pockets and Paine's words in their hearts.[52]

The fame of *Common Sense* reached mythical proportions long ago. The problem is getting a grip on its historical significance. Paine himself estimated that 150,000 copies sold in America during 1776. That is an outrageous claim, one consistent with Paine's ego, but inconsistent with what we know about the technology of printing and the economy of print sales in eighteenth-century America. If we reduce the estimate to 35,000 to 50,000 and admit that, although unlikely, as many as 75,000 copies may have circulated the first year, that is still an extraordinary testament to the pamphlet's success. The twenty-five known American printings is more than double that of any other American book or pamphlet produced before the mid-nineteenth century. In addition, the

---

[51] Corner, *The Autobiography of Benjamin Rush,* 113; Samuel Adams, *Autobiography,* 507; William Temple Franklin, *Memoirs of the Life and Writings of Benjamin Franklin* (London, 1813), 2: 13.

[52] Benjamin Rush to James Cheetham, 17 June 1809, quoted in Keane, *Tom Paine,* 104.

pamphlet's warm reception in France and the multiple British printings made *Common Sense* an international bestseller in its time.[53]

Common Sense was reprinted in fourteen American towns and seven of the thirteen colonies. The first Philadelphia printing of 1,000 copies sold out in a week. When Paine switched publishers in a dispute over royalties, the new printer produced 6,000 copies during February by farming the job out to two printers who split the order. Benjamin Franklin bought 100 copies of the January edition. Robert Aitken purchased eighty for his Philadelphia bookstore during the first month. There were sixteen Philadelphia editions in all, one of them in German.[54]

Although only one edition of *Common Sense* was published south of Philadelphia, in Charleston, South Carolina, and none farther west than Lancaster, Pennsylvania, it was still unprecedented for an American pamphlet to be reprinted outside the region of its origin and in so many places—New York, Hartford, Norwich, Providence, Newport, Salem, Newbury Port, Andover, and Boston. At a time when there was no unifying national identity, except as British, when Americans' cultural and political loyalties were distinctly regional and their prejudices against those outside their region was a defining trait of the colonists, this interregional interest in Thomas Paine's words was simply extraordinary.[55]

In light of Americans' regional parochialism, it is not surprising that it took a foreigner like Paine, a man who had been here for less than a year, to think past regional prejudices. In *Common Sense,* Paine, as an outsider, played the "universal" against the "provincial," always favoring the larger configuration. He instructed the colonists to "get over local or longstanding prejudices." And he used a series of organic metaphors to favor grander linkages and larger relationships as more "natural" than Americans' traditional localism.

> 'Tis not the affair of a city, a country, a province, or a kingdom, but of a continent—of at least one eighth part of the habitable globe. 'Tis not the concern of a day, a year, or an age; posterity are virtually involved in the contest, and will be more or less affected, even to the end of

[53]Trish Loughran, "Disseminating *Common Sense*: The Locations of Print Culture, 1776," unpublished draft of dissertation chapter, University of Chicago.

[54]Ibid.

[55]Richard Gimbel, *Thomas Paine: A Bibliographical Check List of* Common Sense *with an Account of its Publication* (New Haven, 1956).

time, by the proceedings now. Now is the seed time of continental union, faith and honor. The least fracture now will be like a name engraved with the point of a pin on the tender rind of a young oak; the wound will enlarge with the tree, and posterity read it in full grown characters. (Document 6, p. 87)

Paine was trying to build a nation where no tradition of cooperation existed and where the only thing approaching nationalism described Americans' relationship with the "enemy" against whom *Common Sense* encouraged war. That was a central aspect of Paine's genius. He pushed Americans to revolt against their prejudices and their most admired (British) political traditions. He defined for them a new identity as Americans rather than as British colonists, that most of them had only begun groping toward.

Common Sense imagined a continental empire at a time when Americans imagined isolated cities on separate hills. Where Americans feared dispersion and disintegration, Paine championed what many saw as competing ambitions for unity and expansion. The significance of Paine's image of a truly continental nation is immense. It is one of the signal contributions of the pamphlet to American political culture. Americans received this continental ambition with enthusiasm and began to see a continental nation as their destiny, God's will, and their natural right. Thomas Paine wrote *Common Sense* for Americans—not just for Philadelphians, Pennsylvanians, or radical artisans—and inspired colonists to think of themselves as a nation and an empire.

Despite the unprecedented number of interregional publications, the huge sales, the public controversy it generated, and the enthusiastic reception by radicals, no one made money on *Common Sense*. The costs of production were too high, and the market outside Philadelphia too scattered. Paine died in debt to his first publisher for the production costs of the pamphlet. Calling the pamphlet a bestseller is also slightly misleading. Most often leading revolutionaries, like Franklin, gave away copies of *Common Sense*.[56]

Still, as many as 20,000 copies of *Common Sense* may have circulated in Philadelphia alone. Philadelphia was America's largest, most cosmopolitan city, and with a population of 30,000 it was the third largest city in the British Empire. It was America's fastest growing city, the population doubling between 1750 and 1770, and it was America's busiest port, its most bustling mercantile center. It was also America's

[56] Ibid.

William Birch, *Second Street North from Market Street,* Philadelphia. Engravings, 1799.
I. N. Phelps Stokes Collection, Miriam and Ira D. Wallach Division of Art, Prints and Photographs, The New York Public Library, Astor, Lennox and Tilden Foundations.

most heterogeneous city, with a mix of Quakers, Anglicans, Catholics, German Lutherans, Mennonites, and Scots-Irish Presbyterians.[57]

Philadelphia was also a city seriously divided over relations with England. *Common Sense* was a catalyst for such conflict, which is precisely what Paine intended. It pushed moderates off the fence and into the polar positions that a revolutionary environment demands. "Though I would carefully avoid giving unnecessary offence," Paine wrote,

> yet I am inclined to believe, that all those who espouse the doctrine of reconciliation, may be included within the following descriptions.

[57] Gary B. Nash, *The Urban Crucible: The Northern Seaports and the Origins of the American Revolution* (Cambridge, Mass., 1979); John J. McCusker and Russell R. Menard, *The Economy of British America* (Chapel Hill, 1985); Thomas M. Doerflinger, *A Vigorous Spirit of Enterprise: Merchants and Economic Development in Revolutionary Philadelphia* (Chapel Hill, 1986).

Interested men, who are not to be trusted; weak men, who *cannot* see; prejudiced men, who *will not* see; and a certain set of moderate men, who think better of the European world than it deserves; and this last class, by an ill-judged deliberation, will be the cause of more calamities to this continent, than all the other three. (p. 91)

His harshest words were reserved for those having a hard time committing to either side. Paine had the least patience with those who intellectualized the situation, rather than following their emotions.

Equality

The radicals were Paine's kind of men. Philadelphia's radical politics had strong links to the very sort of artisan community that had raised Paine, the stay-maker's son. *Common Sense* spoke the language of the artisan classes. Its Bible-based arguments played well among working-class evangelicals. Its calls for "independence" rallied artisans in the language of their social ambitions to be master craftsmen, independent of any man's will. The artisans and *Common Sense* were more democratic than the American mainstream. Their shared faith in both the necessity for and the virtue of personal independence as the basis for governance reflected common ideological roots. Paine's rejection of the past, another hallmark of *Common Sense,* was similarly well received by men of humble origins who strove to better themselves.[58]

Paine's faith in the equality of all men, which combined Quaker influences and working-class ambitions, spoke directly to the artisan's soul. "Male and female are the distinctions of nature," Paine wrote,

good and bad the distinctions of heaven; but how a race of men came into the world so exalted above the rest, and distinguished like some new species, is worth enquiring into, and whether they are the means of happiness or of misery to mankind. (p. 79)

This attack on the perpetual inequality imposed by kingship and the Bible-based defense of independence distinguished *Common Sense*

---

[58]Eric Foner, *Tom Paine and Revolutionary America* (New York, 1976); Christine Leigh Heyerman, *Southern Cross: The Beginnings of the Bible Belt* (New York, 1997); Ronald Schultz, *The Republic of Labor: Philadelphia Artisans and the Politics of Class, 1720–1830* (New York, 1993); Billy G. Smith, "The Material Lives of Laboring Philadelphians, 1750–1800," *William and Mary Quarterly* 3d ser. (1981) 38: 183–200; Smith, *The "Lower Sort": Philadelphia's Laboring People, 1750–1800* (Ithaca, 1990); Sharon V. Salinger, "Artisans, Journeymen, and the Transformation of Labor in Late Eighteenth-Century Philadelphia," *William and Mary Quarterly,* 3d ser. (1983) 40: 62–84; Salinger, *"To Serve Well and Faithfully": Labor and Indentured Servants in Pennsylvania, 1682–1800* (New York, 1987).

from the pamphlets that had come before it.[59] Indeed, one of the most significant differences between *Common Sense* and other Revolutionary-era pamphlets was Paine's elevation of equality over liberty as the highest of political values. His cry for equality spoke for those at the middle and bottom of society. The equality of opportunity and equality before the law that Paine endorsed reflected a more intentionally revolutionary goal than the circumscribed liberty that other writers had in mind.

Biblical Authority

Paine wrote for the American common man, who was both steeped in the Bible and more independently minded than his European counterparts. Paine knew the Bible well, better than most, and he knew that it could be read in more than one way. He understood that arguments couched in biblical authority carried greater weight with believers than those based on mere mortal authority. "Government by kings was first introduced into the world by the Heathens," Paine wrote, "from whom the children of Israel copied the custom. It was the most prosperous invention the Devil ever set on foot for the promotion of idolatry." (p. 79)

In the long passage on monarchy and hereditary succession in *Common Sense* (p. 79), Paine anticipated Bible-based arguments against revolution and countered with alternative readings of the same passages that others might use in defense of monarchy. "These portions of scripture," he concluded, "are direct and positive. They admit of no equivocal construction. That the Almighty hath here entered his protest against monarchical government is true, or the scripture is false." (p. 82) Paine aimed this assault at conservative clergy, who saw the king as ruling by divine right, and who linked God, the monarch, and earthly fathers as occupying parallel positions of authority. This traditional vision of the king and the father as absolute authorities, to whom subjects and children owed perpetual and unquestioned fealty, was under assault in eighteenth-century America. Paine's method and his message reflected an ongoing revolution against patriarchal authority that helped create a receptive environment for Paine's ideas. Those Americans who, like the seventeenth-century English philosopher John Locke, saw both families and government as contractual,

[59]Bernard Bailyn, ed., *Pamphlets of the American Revolution, 1750–1776* (Cambridge, Mass., 1965).

would be open to Paine's suggestion that both King George III and kingship itself were defective in spiritual as well as political ways.[60]

In passages where *Common Sense* referred to the Bible, Paine took a commonplace biblical quotation, such as "Render unto Caesar the things which are Caesar's," which others used to justify their opposition to the Revolution, and stood their argument on its head. That passage, Paine argued, "is no support of monarchical government, for the Jews at that time were without a king, and in a state of vassalage to the Romans." (p. 80) This is a rhetorical device—to use an opponent's authority against him—which Paine called on time and again in *Common Sense,* and used as effectively as any debater of earthly or spiritual issues could. The Bible, which others used to shield monarchy from attack, became in Paine's hands an offensive weapon to fell the whole edifice of logic that supported the British king.

It is also important to keep Paine's religious heritage in mind when reading the letter appended to this edition of *Common Sense.* Paine's remarks are addressed to the Quaker authors of a pamphlet opposing independence. He instructs them on their religion and reprimands them for "dabbling" in politics. In the end, Paine explains that those anonymous authors, who wrapped themselves in the mantle of the Quaker peace testimony—a fundamentally pacifist doctrine—had no more authority to speak for all Quakers than he did, which is to say that they had no authority at all. (p. 115)

Paine dismissed the Quaker authors for misunderstanding both the religious beliefs of the Society of Friends and the political scene around them. He disputed their use of the Bible.

> The quotation which ye have made from Proverbs...that, "when a man's ways please the Lord, he maketh even his enemies to be at peace with him"; is very unwisely chosen on your part; because, it amounts to a proof, that the king's ways (whom ye are so desirous of supporting) do *not* please the Lord, otherwise, his reign would be in peace. (p.117)

He questioned their understanding of the Revolutionary movement. He doubted their commitment to the very religious principles they offered as justification for opposition to the war. "Either ye do not believe what ye profess, or have not virtue enough to practise what ye believe." (p. 118)

---

[60]Jay Fliegelman, *Prodigals and Pilgrims: The American Revolution Against Patriarchal Authority, 1750–1800* (New York, 1982).

Paine's assault on the Quakers took no prisoners. On this score, he was merciless, to be sure, but confident to the core that he knew Quakerism. "Call not coldness of soul, religion; nor put the *Bigot* in the place of the *Christian.*" As a critic, Paine had the certainty of an insider even as he delivered an outsider's lashing of theological rationales for political action. The Quaker signers of the letter claimed, according to Paine, that all they wanted was to

> live a peaceable and quiet life, in all godliness and honesty; *"under the government which God is pleased to set over us."*—If these are *really* your principles why do ye not abide by them? Why do ye not leave that, which ye call God's Work, to be managed by himself? These very principles instruct you to wait with patience and humility, for the event of all public measures, and to receive *that event* as the divine will towards you. (pp. 117–18)

It is interesting that the two religious traditions in which Paine was raised were the ones to which the highest percentage of religiously affiliated Loyalists belonged during the American Revolution. It makes sense to wonder, then, how the tug between his two boyhood religions contributed to Paine's skepticism about all institutional religions and to his impassioned assault on formal linkages between any religion and the state. The Quakers' anti-authoritarianism fit Thomas Paine, and so it is amply displayed in *Common Sense.* Paine also drew on the Anglican ministry's use of biblical texts to support moral arguments. There is a sermonlike structure to these passages, a reasoning from biblical passage to moral argument that is distinctive among political writings of the era, but typical of theological ones from the same time.

Common Sense is ambivalent on the question of whether people are inherently good or evil but Paine's views are consistent with a belief in original sin. If, as Paine wrote, "society is produced by our wants, and government by our wickedness," the wickedness apparently originates in human nature. (p. 74) Government is, or at least should be, designed to "supply the defect of moral virtue" that burdens mankind particularly when we live in society. (p. 75) So, government is necessary to protect us from ourselves.

Although, in Paine's eyes and the Bible's, people are inherently flawed, *Common Sense* found us capable of moral improvement, just as the New Testament does. Indeed, Paine saw eighteenth-century Americans as less corrupted by civilization than Europeans. Americans were inherently good and improvable in the sense that Paine imagined their ethical behavior to win over self-interest in a way that it no longer did in England. The United States would be a young country, and "youth is

the seed time of good habits, as well in nations as in individuals."
(p. 105) Paine saw the Revolution as a moral cause for moral ends, which
is exactly how Americans saw it. Indeed, the urgency that he attached to
an immediate break with England grew directly from his estimation of
America as a more moral society than it would be at a later date.

The Economy of Freedom

Paine's argument was more moral than it was economic, but he
believed that independence would have positive economic consequences, which, in turn, would have beneficial moral effects in American society. Commerce was to Paine, as it was to the Scottish
economic theorists of his day, a liberal and liberating social force. It is
possible that the language Paine used to discuss the morality of capitalism reflected the influence of his Philadelphia friend Benjamin
Rush, who had received his medical training in Scotland where he
became a staunch advocate for such liberal ideas.[61]

In Paine's distinction between government (evil) and society (good),
commerce was clearly an expression of society that was best left alone
by politicians and bureaucrats. Here, Paine identified with those Americans who rebelled against the British government's efforts to regulate
commerce and tax commercial exchanges. He sided with those who
favored rapid and unfettered expansion of a market economy.

> America would have flourished as much, and probably much more, had
> no European power had any thing to do with her. The commerce, by
> which she hath enriched herself are the necessaries of life, and will
> always have a market while eating is the custom of Europe. (p. 87)

Intellectual Influences

Paine's political vision was more ethical than ideological in that *Common Sense* lacked a consistent, coherent ideological structure. For this
reason, intellectual historians find it difficult to locate the influences
for *Common Sense* in the political writings of the great thinkers who
came before Paine. Which is not to say that Paine's ideas were entirely
original. There are many places where he might have gotten his ideas

---

[61] David Freeman Hawke, *Benjamin Rush: Revolutionary Gadfly* (Indianapolis, 1971);
Donald J. D'Elia, "Benjamin Rush: Philosopher of the American Revolution," *Transac-
tions of the American Philosophical Society,* new series (Philadelphia, 1974), 14: 5; Albert
O. Hirschman, *The Passions and the Interests: Political Arguments for Capitalism before
Its Triumph* (Princeton, 1977); Joseph Dorfman, "The Economic Philosophy of Thomas
Paine," *Political Science Quarterly* (1938) 53: 372–86.

about government, society, and the relationship of the present to the past and the future. The problem is identifying the intellectual connections between *Common Sense* and any one philosophical school or the influence of any specific author or text.

Typically, historians and literary critics look first to what an author reads, assuming that written texts are the principal sources for ideas. In the case of Thomas Paine, such searches for intellectual antecedents reveal precious little. There is absolutely no evidence that Paine ever read John Locke—one of the most influential political writers on the American scene—and much of *Common Sense* is inconsistent with Locke's precepts on government and society. For example, Paine's humans were not the blank slates of Locke's *Essay Concerning Human Understanding* (1689) and the highest political value in Locke's *Two Treatises of Government* (1690) is liberty, while Paine's is equality.

Another obvious place to try to locate the ideas of Paine in British political thought is in the works of John Trenchard and Thomas Gordon, the eighteenth-century writers who most influenced other pamphleteers of the Revolutionary era. Again, though, the relationship between the ideas of these "Real Whigs," which were drawn from England's seventeenth-century constitutional revolutions, and Paine's are tenuous at best. Paine never mentioned these men, and there is no evidence that he ever read anything that they wrote.

In significant ways Paine's ideas were in direct conflict with those of the Real Whigs. For example, at the heart of the ideology of the Real Whigs, or eighteenth-century Commonwealthmen as they are sometimes called, was a defense of balanced government. This belief argued that different interests in society are reflected best in the very structure of government, as in the House of Lords' representation of British nobility and the House of Commons' representation of the property-owning middling classes of Great Britain. The British constitution seemed to the Real Whigs and to their American followers to balance these contending forces—monarchy, aristocracy, and property-owning commoners—in ways that protected an ever-fragile liberty from the encroachments of anarchy, oligarchy, and tyranny. Paine, on the other hand, denounced the complexity of balanced government and favored a simpler, more democratic model.[62]

---

[62] Caroline Robbins, *The Eighteenth-Century Commonwealthman: Studies in the Transmission, Development and Circumstance of English Liberal Thought from the Restoration of Charles II until the War with the Thirteen Colonies* (Cambridge, England,

When eighteenth-century Americans discussed politics in the pamphlets that preceded *Common Sense,* they revealed their loyalty to the British constitution as it was described by John Locke and the Real Whigs. Americans' ideas about balanced government also reflected their Enlightenment sensibilities, their distinctive brand of Whig ideology, and their capitalist experiences and values. They conceived of governance as something of a balancing act among the few and the many, the rich and the propertied middling sort, the powerful and the weak. They imagined a delicate scale with liberty on one side and order on the other. Too much weight on either side, they believed, could bring disarray to the political world—anarchy if the masses ran amok, oligarchy and ultimately tyranny if the rulers became corrupted by power.

Paine, in a truly revolutionary departure from the intellectual origins of the American Revolution, attacked the British constitution rather than argue, as previous pamphleteers had, a simple lack of balance and the need to protect liberty against conspiring tyrants. Paine declared monarchy the problem, not just a particular monarch and his circle of advisors. *Common Sense* indicted the very concept of a balanced constitution and argued for revolt against the structure of government that Americans revered.

So, Paine turned neither to the political philosophers revered by Americans nor to the traditions of Anglo-American politics for the intellectual underpinnings of *Common Sense.* He wrote against history and tradition; he attacked received wisdom as the enemy. Paine drew heavily on his own life, his witness to injustice, the moral and religious education of his youth, and the radical politics of his class and profession. And, not least of all, he drew from his boyhood days in the Wilderness for a natural philosophy that is uniquely his.

Paine's affection for nature is woven into *Common Sense.* This quintessential urban revolutionary was a country boy at heart. His literary

---

1959); J. G. A. Pocock, *The Ancient Constitution and the Feudal Law: English Historical Thought in the Seventeenth Century* (Cambridge, England, 1957); Bernard Bailyn, *The Ideological Origins of American Politics* (Cambridge, 1967). On Paine's ideas not fitting with those of other eighteenth-century political philosophers, including Rousseau and Montesquieu, see Alfred Own Aldridge, *Thomas Paine's American Ideology* (Newark, Del., 1984); J. G. A. Pocock, *Virtue Commerce and History: Essays on Political Thought and History, Chiefly in the Eighteenth Century* (Cambridge, England, 1985), 276; Pocock, "Political Thought in the English-Speaking Atlantic, 1760–1790, Part 1: The Imperial Crisis," in Pocock, ed., *The Varieties of British Political Thought, 1500–1800* (Cambridge, England, 1993), 279–80, 282.

triumphs as an adult came in cities, but the soul of his writing was in woodland and field. The logical places to look for Paine's naturalism in *Common Sense* are those passages that address natural rights. For Paine, the link between "nature" and "natural" was more than linguistic, and discussion of what was natural (rights) and unnatural (kings) revealed the influence of the heath. In the introduction to *Common Sense,* "Nature" has an uppercase *N.* Paine heard the "voice of nature" (p. 76), felt "injuries which nature cannot forgive" (p. 99), and drew his "idea of the form of government from a principle of nature." (p. 76) He called on the authority of nature with the same assurance that he quoted the Bible; and he knew as surely as he knew a moral wrong when he saw it that "nature" would be on America's side in its war for independence. Such language came from Paine's heart and spoke clearly to a people hewing their way through a continental wilderness of their own. When we seek the connections that made *Common Sense* so appealing to so many Americans, their shared naturalism should be on our list.

Propaganda

The mass appeal of *Common Sense* was also as much a product of Paine's method as it was his message. It was as much how he said it as it was what he said. Paine showed what he was up to by reading passages aloud to his friend Benjamin Rush as he drafted the pamphlet. He intended for most people to hear *Common Sense* rather than to read it. We know that people borrowed and lent copies. People reported public readings in taverns and out of doors. Because most people who got the message got it aurally, we need to consider the pamphlet as a dramatic script.

The phrasing, cadences, and emotionality of passages probably made more of an impression to the listening audience than the relationship between argument and evidence, because Paine's logic is not the great strength of *Common Sense.* Paine's message is reflected in his style. In this regard, it is difficult to imagine a text less similar to *Common Sense* than Thomas Jefferson's draft of the Declaration of Independence, which is full of long, flowing, complex sentences that reason doggedly from assertion, to evidence, to conclusion. While Jefferson's style is intellectually powerful, Paine's is emotionally hot.[63]

[63] Jay Fliegelman, *Declaring Independence: Jefferson, Natural Language, and the Culture of Performance* (Stanford, 1993); Derek Jarrett, *England in the Age of Hogarth* (London, 1974).

Paine was not a profound thinker, an innovative philosopher, or a grand architect of institutions. When the Founding Fathers drafted a constitution for the United States, they turned neither to the principles nor the institutional models of *Common Sense*. Instead, they returned to the Real Whigs' notions of balanced and separated powers, restoring to the American government the very complexity of the British Constitution that Paine decried in *Common Sense*.

And yet, the domestic appeal of *Common Sense* was, if anything, wider than the Constitution's during the eighteenth century and not less than that of the Declaration of Independence through the end of the war. With inspiring cadences punctuated by strong words and jarring illustrations, Paine intended to move his audience emotionally rather than intellectually. Read, for example, the following passage aloud:

> Here then is the origin and rise of government; namely, a mode rendered necessary by the inability of moral virtue to govern the world; here too is the design and end of government, viz. freedom and security. And however our eyes may be dazzled with show, or our ears deceived by sound; however prejudice may warp our wills, or interest darken our understanding, the simple voice of nature and of reason will say, it is right. (p. 76)

No doubt about it, this passage sounds good. It builds to a crescendo of emotion that is moving to hear and thrilling to read aloud. Paine wanted his prose to be accessible. His goal was to provide "simple facts, plain arguments, and common sense" (p. 86) to show those with open minds what habit and prejudice had blinded them to thus far. But he wanted to do much more than convince. He wanted to move readers to action. That ambition put *Common Sense* in the category of propaganda, so we need to think about Paine's goals and techniques within the context of other eighteenth-century attempts to move people emotionally in support of shared goals.

In many ways, *Common Sense* had more in common with the visual propaganda of its day than with other pamphlets written on the American struggle with Great Britain. Exaggeration, caricature, and confrontation were the defining techniques of both the pamphlet and the century's stellar examples of visual propaganda. Paine moved the political pamphlet from the realm of reasoned intellectual appeal to a small group of like-minded, well-educated, upper-class men, to the sort of mass appeal that the English engraver William Hogarth sought to achieve.

William Hogarth, *Gin Lane,* 1750, London street scene illustrating the social problems associated with gin consumption.
The Library Company of Philadelphia.

William Hogarth's (1697–1764) "Gin Lane" is widely recognized as one of the most effective pieces of social reform propaganda ever produced. It was aimed at reforming the English laws on unlicensed sale of gin. Hogarth, like Paine, intended to shock his audience. He aimed at people's guts rather than their heads. He exaggerated—even the buildings seem drunk. He inflamed. He yelled rather than reasoned about a social problem that demanded immediate attention. Rather than render a literal truth about the state of London in 1750 when the print appeared, he predicted a future horrible to contemplate.

Hogarth made a moral judgment. The prominent emotion is rage, but there are others as well—pity, sadness, and even humor. Most of all, though, he was angry—furious, outraged; and he wanted those who saw "Gin Lane" to share his emotions. His style was accessible like Paine's, colloquial, even bawdy, rather than refined, affected, and polished by polite social and artistic conventions. Hogarth's style both delivered and embodied the print's message. The bare breast, the skewered child, and the skeletal corpse were intended to shock. He wanted the visual story he told to disturb—anger, embarrass, unsettle—viewers. Keep Hogarth's imagery in mind as you begin reading Paine's pamphlet. Remember particularly "Gin Lane's" focused rage and stylistic exaggeration when considering *Common Sense,* a moral tale replete with language intended to move readers emotionally toward revolutionary action.[64]

THE FORESTER

Common Sense angered those who sought reconciliation with Great Britain, infuriated those who favored a middle course, and even scared some ardent American patriots. Paine responded to the conservatives and conciliators during 1776 in four essays that he signed "The Forester." The origin of the pseudonym remains obscure, but it clearly reflects Paine's naturalism and perhaps an image of his task. Possibly Paine saw himself as winnowing dead wood, clearing the political forest of the weak limbed, so that the sturdy trees might prosper in a healthier environment.

These exchanges between Paine and his published critics lack the fire and imagination of *Common Sense* and played to the much smaller audience of Pennsylvania's political elite. They read more like the thrusts of hand-to-hand combat—quibbles over the meanings of quoted sources, accusations of indiscretion, and parries over style as well as content—than the loud blast that occasioned the fuss. The essays are, nonetheless, significant for what they reveal about divisions among the revolutionaries

---

[64]Foner, *Tom Paine and Revolutionary America,* 5; Bernard Bailyn, "Thomas Paine," *Faces of Revolution: Personalities and Themes in the Struggle for American Independence* (New York, 1990), 67–84.

themselves and for the ways they capture the issues that defined those troubled times.

John Adams was among the patriots who found *Common Sense* disturbing. The Massachusetts lawyer, who would become the second president of the United States, composed his *Thoughts on Government* in response to what he read as the dangerously democratic tendencies of *Common Sense.* Adams and other conservative patriots feared that a war for independence from Great Britain would unleash a social revolution in America. They imagined with horror the sort of bloody internal violence and class conflict that would threaten the property, interests, and persons of the wealthiest and best educated Americans. "I dreaded the effect so popular a pamphlet might have among the people," Adams wrote, "and determined to do all in my power, to counteract the effect of it."[65]

The four "Forester" letters were Paine's only sustained response to critics of *Common Sense.* They were an assault on "Cato," an anonymous critic whose letters appeared in Pennsylvania newspapers. Paine intended to reduce the "hypocrite" to matchsticks by chopping away at Cato's integrity, accusing him of "falsehoods and fallacious reasonings," cowardice, and of being "an enemy to mankind." (Document 7, p. 122)

Because style was essential to Paine's task, Cato's style became a target for ridicule. "The first of Cato's letters is insipid," Paine wrote, "in its stile, language and substance." (p. 122) Cato, as Paine portrayed him, represented the opposite of what he congratulated himself and *Common Sense* for being—bold, manly, honest, global in its vision, and powerful in its prose. Cato was "insipid," "hypocritical," provincial, corrupt, barbaric, and "savage."

This was local politics being fought out tooth and nail. Indeed, Paine argued, that was precisely the problem with Cato. He lacked a national vision. He could see the issues only from a very narrow local perspective. His remarks were "crouded with personal and private innuendues" (p. 122) that marked him as both an enemy of the people of Pennsylvania and of the larger American community that Paine had sought to build with *Common Sense.*

There were also, though, flashes of Paine's electrifying prose. Master of beginnings that he was, Paine again opened with a rhetorical flourish reminiscent of his best writing.

To be *nobly wrong* is more manly than to be *meanly right.* Only let the error be disinterested—let it wear, *not the mask,* but the *mark* of principle and 'tis pardonable. It is on this large and liberal ground, that we

---

[65]Adams quoted in Foner, *Tom Paine and Revolutionary America,* 122.

distinguish between men and their tenets, and generously preserve our friendship for the one, while we combat with every prejudice of the other. (p. 120)

Paine's use of italics to highlight the reversal of assumptions—that it could be better to be wrong than right—and the high moral tone mark this passage and the rest of the Forester letters as Paine's. But there is also a negative, defensive quality to the Forester essays that does not show Paine at his best. At the top of his form, Paine was on the attack. He was not patient, careful, or gracious. As a writer, Paine was a man of action better at surprise assault than at defending his bunker.

RADICAL POLITICS

Even as he slashed at the critics behind him, Paine thrust himself forward into the radical politics of Pennsylvania during 1776. He supported adding delegates to the state assembly from the underrepresented western counties and Philadelphia, which would make the state more democratic in precisely the ways that Adams and others feared. Paine campaigned for radical delegates in Philadelphia's local elections, but his efforts were largely frustrated and only three moderates and one radical delegate that he supported were elected.[66]

Pennsylvania's Constitutional Convention produced, also in 1776, a document that is generally acknowledged as the most radically democratic frame of government to come out of the Revolutionary era. The new constitution rejected the idea of balanced government, instead providing for a single-house legislature and replacing the governor with a weak, veto-less, and plural executive council directly elected by the people. It also established annual elections, rotation of officeholders, and legislative debates open to the public. It eliminated property qualifications for officeholders and extended voting rights to all free men over the age of twenty-one who paid taxes.[67]

---

[66]Foner, *Tom Paine and Revolutionary America,* chap. 4; Richard Alan Ryerson, *The Revolution Is Now Begun: The Radical Committees of Philadelphia, 1765–1776* (Philadelphia, 1978), chap. 7; Robert L. Brunhouse, *The Counter-Revolution in Pennsylvania, 1776–1790* (New York, 1942), chap. 2; Anne M. Ousterhout, *A State Divided: Opposition in Pennsylvania to the American Revolution* (Westport, Conn., 1987), chap. 4.

[67]J. Paul Selsam, *The Pennsylvania Constitution of 1776: A Study in Revolutionary Democracy* (Philadelphia, 1936); Willi Paul Adams, *The First American Constitutions: Republican Ideology and the Making of the State Constitutions in the Revolutionary Era* (Chapel Hill, 1980); Gordon S. Wood, *The Creation of the American Republic, 1776–1787* (Chapel Hill, 1969); J. R. Pole, *Political Representation in England and the Origins of the American Republic* (London, 1966).

This was a frame of government fully inspired by Paine's principles. Simple, "natural" government unburdened by the complexities of balance and a strong, independent executive. It was democratic in the same ways and abided by the same limits that Paine outlined in *Common Sense.* Suffrage was extended to all "independent" men, but no farther. This was the kind of democracy that Adams, among the conservatives on both sides of the Revolution's divide, feared.

Paine was not in Philadelphia when the convention met. He volunteered for the state militia and agreed to serve as secretary without pay to General Daniel Roberdeau. In the fall, when Roberdeau's command disbanded, Paine was appointed aide-de-camp to General Nathaniel Greene at Fort Lee, New Jersey. He also wrote dispatches to Philadelphia newspapers reporting on the course of the war.[68]

THE AMERICAN CRISIS

Paine was with Generals George Washington and Nathaniel Greene when the army retreated from New York to Newark, leaving behind cooking stoves, boiling pots, and 300 tents in their hasty departure. While in Newark Paine began work on *The American Crisis.* The American army was on the run and Paine's intention to complete the essay for publication in New Jersey fell victim to the rout. The war was going badly for Washington's army, to say the least. Hungry, cold, exhausted, and demoralized, more than half either deserted or simply declined to reenlist when their commitment expired. "Your imagination can scarce extend to a situation more distressing than mine," Washington wrote to a relative on December 17.

> Our only dependence now is upon the speedy enlistment of a new army. If this fails, I think the game will be pretty well up, as from disaffection and want of spirit and fortitude, the inhabitants, instead of resistance, are offering submission and taking protection from Gen. Howe in Jersey.[69]

General Washington's army moved south quickly, some would say precipitously, and crossed the Delaware River into Pennsylvania. At this point Paine left his post and began walking to Philadelphia. He

---

[68] Greene quoted in Moncure Daniel Conway, *The Life of Thomas Paine,* 2 vols. (New York, 1893), 1: 82–83.

[69] George Washington to Lund Washington, December 17, 1776, quoted in Conway, *Life of Thomas Paine,* 1: 84.

covered the twenty-three miles on foot, wary about what the British might do to him if he were captured, especially when they found the manuscript in his pocket. Tired, hungry, cold, and scared, he reached Philadelphia without incident and published the first of *The American Crisis* essays on December 19. Eighteen thousand copies appeared in pamphlet form and it was widely reprinted in newspapers across the country. When copies reached the army, Washington read it and ordered the pamphlet read to his troops on the eve of recrossing the Delaware for the Battle of Trenton.[70]

Paine's literary lightning struck again. As with *Common Sense* the significance of the first *Crisis* essay was a combination of writing genius and brilliant timing. This was the stuff of which myths are born. Bedraggled, demoralized troops standing in small groups assembled in the biting winter cold on the Pennsylvania riverbank, awestruck and inspired by Paine's words. Steeling themselves for battle, the soldiers then recrossed the icy Delaware River on small barges. Now both wet and cold, Washington's troops marched with a new determination to their first major victory at Trenton, followed by another at Princeton, an essential turning point of the war. Here are the legendary opening words, which again must be read aloud to capture their full impact, to imagine their effect on the men who heard them under such bitter circumstances.

> These are the times that try men's souls: The summer soldier and the sunshine patriot will, in this crisis, shrink from the service of his country; but he that stands it NOW, deserves the love and thanks of man and woman. Tyranny, like hell, is not easily conquered; yet we have this consolation with us, that the harder the conflict, the more glorious the triumph. What we obtain too cheap, we esteem too lightly: — 'Tis dearness only that gives every thing its value. Heaven knows how to set a proper price upon its goods; and it would be strange indeed, if so celestial an article as FREEDOM should not be highly rated. Britain, with an army to enforce her tyranny, has declared, that she has a right (*not only to* TAX) but "*to* BIND *us in* ALL CASES WHATSOEVER," and if being *bound in that manner* is not slavery, then is there not such a thing as slavery upon earth. Even the expression is impious, for so unlimited a power can belong only to GOD. (Document 8, p. 126)

The language is stunning; the effect is inspiring; even two centuries away from the moment it can still produce goose bumps. "These are

---

[70]Keane, *Tom Paine,* 141–45.

the times that try men's souls" is one of the two most famous opening lines in all of English literature; the other is Charles Dickens's "It was the best of times, it was the worst of times" in *A Tale of Two Cities*.[71] Paine's "summer soldier and the sunshine patriot" invented language that we now take for granted. "What we esteem too cheap, we esteem too lightly" delivered folksy wisdom to the common man in a style that could inspire generals as well as privates. Again, as with *Common Sense,* it was less the content than it was the delivery that made this *Crisis* essay one of the enduring works of American literature.

The parallels to *Common Sense* are both fascinating and instructive. Paine used some of the devices that he had already employed in earlier writings. The selective use of capitalization highlights the concepts that Paine wanted to shout—NOW, FREEDOM, TAX, BIND, and GOD. He italicized words to focus and slow the performer at key passages that demanded particular emphasis. He continued this pattern throughout the *Crisis* series. He again used contrasting opposites that set alternatives in bold relief—man and woman, freedom and slavery, and summer and winter. The call on God as arbiter of the righteousness of the American cause, the claim of the moral high ground in the conflict, and the accompanying implication that Americans are a chosen people were asserted again.

Paine's task as a propagandist was similar to that of a year earlier, but even more daunting. Having argued in *Common Sense* that Americans could not lose in a war with Great Britain, he now had to convince them that they could win. He reminded Americans that this was a war of good versus evil and that, therefore, only atheists could imagine a British victory.

> Neither have I so much of the infidel in me, as to suppose, that HE has relinquished the government of the world, and given us up to the care of devils; and as I do not, I cannot see on what grounds the king of Britain can look up to heaven for help against us. A common murderer, a highwayman, or a housebreaker, has as good a pretence as he. (p. 127)

Paine demonized the enemy. He steadfastly portrayed the war as defensive. Americans had the same right, indeed the same duty, to defend themselves against an "invasion" as they did to protect their families against burglars.

---

[71] Charles Dickens, *A Tale of Two Cities* (London, 1859; Folio Society, 1985), 1.

The *American* CRISIS.

NUMBER I.

By the Author of COMMON SENSE.

THESE are the times that try men's fouls: The fummer foldier and the funfhine patriot will, in this crifis, fhrink from the fervice of his country; but he that ftands it NOW, deferves the love and thanks of man and woman. Tyranny, like hell, is not eafily conquered; yet we have this confolation with us, that the harder the conflict, the more glorious the triumph. What we obtain too cheap, we efteem too lightly:---'Tis dearnefs only that gives every thing its value. Heaven knows how to fet a proper price upon its goods; and it would be ftrange indeed, if fo celeftial an article as FREEDOM fhould not be highly rated. Britain, with an army to enforce her tyranny, has declared, that fhe has a right *(not only to* TAX*)* but "*to* BIND *us in* ALL CASES WHATSOEVER," and if being *bound in that manner* is not flavery, then is there not fuch a thing as flavery upon earth. Even the expreffion is impious, for fo unlimited a power can belong only to GOD.

WHETHER the Independence of the Continent was declared too foon, or delayed too long, I will not now enter into as an argument; my own fimple opinion is, that had it been eight months earlier, it would have been much better. We did not make a proper ufe of laft winter, neither could we, while we were in a dependent ftate. However, the fault, if it were one, was all our own; we have none to blame but ourfelves*. But no great deal is loft yet; all that Howe has been doing for this month paft is rather a ravage than a conqueft, which the fpirit of the Jerfies a year ago would have quickly repulfed, and which time and a little refolution will foon recover.

I have as little fuperftition in me as any man living, but my

---

* " The prefent winter" (meaning the laft) " is worth an " age, if rightly employed, but if loft, or neglected, the whole " Continent will partake of the evil; and there is no punifh- " ment that man does not deferve, be he who, or what, or " where he will, that may be the means of facrificing a feafon " fo precious and ufeful." COMMON SENSE.

Blood-stained title page of the first pamphlet edition of *The American Crisis, Number 1,* published December 1776.
American Philosophical Society.

The king was a crook and his soldiers were hoodlums, Paine reminded the American troops. The fate of their families hung in the balance and the stakes were of the highest importance. If, God forbid, the British were to win, the consequences would include a "ravaged" countryside, "depopulated" cities, and "slavery without hope—our homes turned into barracks and baudy-houses for Hessians." (p. 132) Paine's imagery included the rape of loved ones, who became the slaves and prostitutes of the German soldiers from the province of Hesse, who fought for England's king. Whether the American soldier who heard these words hailed from the country or city, the imagery of destruction was addressed directly to him.

The troops under General Washington had not failed us, Paine explained. They were brave and manly, but they were victims of circumstances that included the enemy's greater numbers and the disloyalty of Americans, particularly in New Jersey. Greater support for the war effort and harsher dealing with traitors were the remedies that Paine recommended. Confiscate the property of the cowardly, treasonous Tories both to punish them and to finance the war. Let the Tories know that the British could not protect them and that their betrayal would come at a price.

> America could carry on a two years war by the confiscation of the property of disaffected persons, and be made happy by their expulsion. Say not that this is revenge, call it rather the soft resentment of a suffering people, who, having no object in view but the GOOD of ALL, have staked their OWN ALL upon a seemingly doubtful event. (p. 130)

Most important, Paine told his listeners, do not be discouraged by the losses of the Revolution's first year. They were understandable and easily reversed; "A single successful battle next year will settle the whole." (p. 130) Paine's confidence, if sincere, was mistaken. Even with the early victories of 1777 and the rout of British troops at Saratoga later in the year, the war would continue for another six long years. Paine's point, though, was that Americans needed to focus on the morality of their cause, their virtue as a people, and that God was on their side. "'Tis the business of little minds to shrink," Paine wrote, "but he whose heart is firm, and whose conscience approves his conduct, will pursue his principles unto death." (p. 131)

The "single successful battle" that Americans would win at Trenton shortly after the publication of Paine's essay proved him right in one important sense, though. The British could be beaten by Americans. Washington's troops, encouraged by Paine and that victory, would reenlist and fight on for what they termed their "glorious cause." Paine, as much as any one person, inspired that mythic understanding of America's triumph and encouraged them to find victory even in apparent defeat. The winter at Valley Forge the following year, for example, was a brutal experience for the men who survived it, but it honed the moral edge that Paine forged with *Common Sense* and *The Crisis*. As much as anyone else in that first year of Revolution, Paine defined the moral enterprise upon which the United States became based.[72]

THOMAS PAINE'S FUTURE

For Thomas Paine, *Common Sense* and the first number of *The American Crisis* were far from the end of his brilliant and controversial career as a propagandist. The other twelve numbers of the *Crisis* series were a major contribution to waging the long war. The war's end in 1783 left Paine unemployed as a political revolutionary, but full of revolutionary ideas, which he pursued with his usual vigor. He wrote on banking and other monetary issues as Americans debated how to finance their newly won freedom. He worked on inventions that satisfied his practical, scientific bent, most notably smokeless candles and a model for a single-arch, wrought-iron bridge. He accepted membership in the American Philosophical Society, which recognized his contributions as both a writer and an inventor. And, as many accomplished immigrants did, Paine returned home, craving his homeland's belated recognition of his genius.[73]

In England during the late 1780s, Paine visited his mother in Thetford, providing her with financial security in her old age. His father had died in 1786, one year before the son's triumphant return. Paine also exhibited the model of his iron bridge in London and Paris and helped in the creation of a real one by an English foundry. In Paris, in 1789, he

---

[72]Robert Middlekauff, *The Glorious Cause: The American Revolution, 1763–1789* (New York, 1982).
[73]Keane, *Tom Paine*, 267–82.

met and became friends with America's new ambassador, Thomas Jefferson, and Jefferson's good friend, the Marquis de Lafayette, who had fought in America's revolution and was now engaged in the beginning of another in France. In London, Paine also met Edmund Burke, the well-known British writer and politician. When Burke published his famous tract *Reflections on the Revolution in France* (1789), Paine was again in the right place at the right time to engage in a literary battle with huge social and political implications.[74]

Burke's *Reflections* sold 12,000 copies in London in its first month. Paine's response to it, *Rights of Man: Being an Answer to Mr. Burke's Attack on the French Revolution,* followed in a matter of weeks and stirred up a maelstrom unlike anything since *Common Sense.* As Paine later described *Rights of Man,* it was a revolutionary pamphlet modeled on *Common Sense,* which brought the same principles across the ocean for a similar set of circumstances, with differences particular to time and place. He had changed his mind about nothing significant and inspired the French with his advocacy of simplicity, natural rights, and the evil of monarchy. More than 200,000 copies sold in Paris during 1792 alone.

The *Rights of Man* made Paine wildly popular in some French circles and earned him infamy back in England for taking the enemy's side. Crowds in London hanged and burned Paine's effigy, and the British government attempted to suppress sale of the pamphlet by prosecuting printers and sellers. Paine himself was indicted for seditious libel, but in absentia, because he had the good sense to remain in France.

In Paris, Paine became deeply involved in Revolutionary politics, despite the handicap of not being able to speak or read French when he arrived there. He remained a bit slow and muddled in his responses to the huge shifts of sentiment that occurred frequently and ferociously, and he was caught off guard when arrests and executions reached his political comrades. When the French king, Louis XVI, was convicted of treason, Paine advised a pardon. When Louis was beheaded on January 21, 1793, Paine attempted to withdraw from French politics and began drinking heavily. At this point, during the fall of 1793, Paine started working on the first part of *The Age of Reason,* his deistic view of religion, which was an assault on biblical authority, organized religion, and the divinity of Christ.[75]

---

[74] Ibid.
[75] Georges Lefebvre, *The French Revolution,* trans. Elizabeth Moss Evanson, 2 vols. (New York, 1962).

In the last days of 1793, Paine was arrested, as the French Revolution took yet another turn that he did not fully comprehend. In jail he worried, grew ill and bitter, and was truly in danger of execution. Being Thomas Paine, though, he also wrote, completing *The Age of Reason,* his most controversial work of all.

Whether Paine had changed his mind about the Bible's authority since 1776 or had simply played to his Bible-based American audience for other ends is a good question, and not easily answered. It is clear, though, that by 1794, when *The Age of Reason* was published, Paine's naturalism dominated both his politics and his religion. Like Benjamin Franklin and Thomas Jefferson, it was nature's God to whom Paine prayed. He believed in the wisdom, but not the divinity of Jesus Christ. As a deist, Paine believed that the creator of the universe put nature in motion but did not tinker with the natural model whose laws now ruled. Paine was far from the atheist whom his enemies denounced, but not the Christian that both of his parents had been.

Just short of a year after his arrest, Paine was released from prison, but was afraid to leave France in case the ship that he sailed on would be captured by the British, whom he believed would jail him on his seditious-libel conviction. So, he remained on the fringes of French politics and society, and he wrote. He wrote about politics (*Dissertation on First Principles of Government,* 1795), religion (the second part of *The Age of Reason,* which contains his most vociferous attack on the Bible, 1795), capitalism (*The Decline and Fall of the English System of Finance,* 1796), and social injustice (*Agrarian Justice,* 1797).

Paine longed to return to America, but had done a pretty good job of burning bridges there, too. The French Revolution was widely perceived as excessively violent in just the ways that John Adams and others had feared the American Revolution would be. The Federalists were in ascendance and a conservative counterreaction to the most liberal and radical ambitions of the American Revolution was fighting a rearguard action during the presidencies of Washington and John Adams, who were more sympathetic to English than French politics during the 1790s. In sum, Paine and radical politics were decidedly out of fashion in an America that had largely put the more radical implications of its own revolution behind it.[76]

Thomas Jefferson was then inaugurated as the third president of the United States in 1801. Jefferson had a literary radical streak

---

[76]James Roger Sharp, *American Politics in the Early Republic: The New Nation in Crisis* (New Haven, 1993).

Nineteenth-century image of Thomas Paine at window of a house
in Herring Street, now Bleecker Street, Greenwich Village, New
York, where he resided from 1808 until his death in 1809.
American Philosophical Society.

himself; he had written in theoretical support of revolutions in general, supported the French Revolution, and was himself a deist. During
the first month of his presidency, Jefferson wrote to Paine and invited
him back to the United States, offering passage on an American warship. Paine awaited the right opportunity, still fearing capture by the
British, who routinely boarded American ships on the high seas. He
finally left Le Havre in September 1802, arriving in Baltimore on October 30. Despite newspaper attacks on Paine for his religious views,

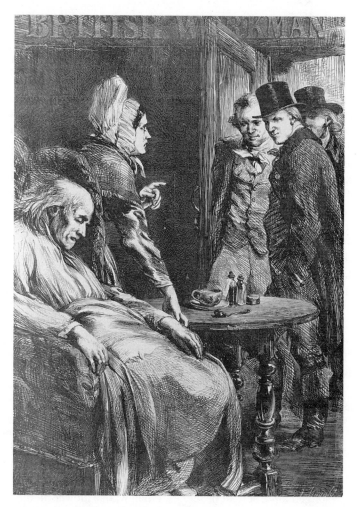

John Gilbert, *The Last Moments of Tom Paine.*
Courtesy of the Thetford Library, Norfolk.

describing him as a drunk and atheist, Jefferson received him in the White House in a show of personal support that must have warmed Paine's heart.

Paine did not make things easier on himself, though, and soon published a series of letters "To the Citizens of the United States," in which he attacked John Adams and described the late President George Washington as a bad general and chief executive. Old friends Samuel Adams and Benjamin Rush refused even to see him because of their disdain for *The Age of Reason*.[77]

Paine's views on religion, his association with the French Revolution, and published descriptions of him as a drunk and a lecher made this once-celebrated American revolutionary first unpopular, and then ignored. He was just too radical for the new nation he had helped to create. So, Paine moved to a farm in New Rochelle, New York, in 1803, grew ill and drank heavily. Not only had he been greeted by a hostile crowd when passing through Trenton, New Jersey, on his way north, but election officials in New Rochelle insulted him by questioning his citizenship and declining to count his vote. In 1806, Paine moved to Manhattan. In 1808, he boarded at a house in Greenwich Village. As he neared the end of his life, Paine was in agony from gout, an excruciating inflammation of the joints, which led him to self-medicate with increasing quantities of liquor. He also lost the use of his legs from a combination of the gout and injuries he suffered falling down a flight of stairs when he had a stroke in 1806.

In January 1809, Paine made out his will. At this point he required constant medical care. He had developed severe swelling and painful skin sores. The Society of Friends denied his request to be buried in a Quaker cemetery. He refused public pleas to recant his deism and accept Christianity before his death. He died on June 9. Only six people attended his funeral in New York and he was buried on his New Rochelle farm. His death passed virtually unnoticed in the American press.

Ten years later, in 1819, the English journalist William Cobbett had Paine's bones exhumed and shipped to England. Cobbett intended to have a public memorial built to Paine, but the plan failed and the bones were eventually lost. Perhaps that is a fitting, if unfortunate, end for a true revolutionary. When Paine's moment, indeed moments, were past there was no comfortable place for such a restless radical, who never truly belonged anywhere at peace. As a man whose life was in the words he wrote against the past and for the revolutionary moment, Paine embodied an uncomfortable presence to the defenders of the status quo wherever he lived. His words live for those who restlessly look to the future rather than the past for solutions to political and social ills. His ideas survive among those who believe that the present is better than the past, and who hope for a future that is freer, simpler, more just, and more responsible to nature than the world into which they are born.[78]

[77] Catherine L. Albanese, *Nature Religion in America: From the Algonkian Indians to the New Age* (Chicago, 1990).
[78] Keane, *Tom Paine,* chap. 12.

PART TWO

The Documents

1

African Slavery in America

1774

Paine wrote this essay only a few weeks after he arrived in Philadelphia, probably before the end of December 1774. It was published in the Pennsylvania Journal *on March 8, 1775. Ironically, in the same issue of the* Journal *an advertisement offered "a stout healthy negro man" for sale. That slave was one of about 6,000 in Pennsylvania. Quakers, who were a significant presence in the colony, were ridding themselves of slaves, a long process begun in the last years of the seventeenth century and completed in 1776. Pamphlets had appeared attacking the slave trade — an anonymous pamphlet in 1762, another by the Quaker Anthony Benezet in 1767, and a third by Dr. Benjamin Rush in 1772. Others spoke against slavery and the slave trade, including the New Jersey Quaker John Woolman, but Paine's was among the first antislavery, as opposed to anti-slave trade, writings published in Pennsylvania.*

The essay's rhetoric is vintage Paine. Its vocabulary of invective, pity, and ridicule is found in most of Paine's later work. The dual appeal of

Moncure Daniel Conway, *The Writings of Thomas Paine,* 2 vols. (New York: G. P. Putnam's Sons, 1894): 1, 4–9.

logic and emotion, to the hearts and souls of readers, is in Common
Sense, *too. Paine's rage is also here, his take-no-prisoners indictment of
those who perpetrate evil, his assault on the unnatural in nature's name,
and his call on Christianity to wage a holy war against immorality.*

Messrs. BRADFORD,
   Please to insert the following, and oblige yours

                                   A. B.

To AMERICANS.

THAT some desperate wretches should be willing to steal and
enslave men by violence and murder for gain, is rather lamentable
than strange. But that many civilized, nay, christianized people should
approve, and be concerned in the savage practice, is surprising; and
still persist, though it has been so often proved contrary to the light of
nature, to every principle of Justice and Humanity, and even good policy, by a succession of eminent men,* and several late publications.

Our Traders in MEN *(an unnatural commodity!)* must know the
wickedness of that SLAVE-TRADE, if they attend to reasoning, or the dictates of their own hearts; and such as shun and stiffle all these, wilfully
sacrifice Conscience, and the character of integrity to that golden Idol.

The Managers of that Trade themselves, and others, testify, that
many of these African nations inhabit fertile countries, are industrious
farmers, enjoy plenty, and lived quietly, averse to war, before the Europeans debauched them with liquors, and bribing them against one
another; and that these inoffensive people are brought into slavery, by
stealing them, tempting Kings to sell subjects, which they can have no
right to do, and hiring one tribe to war against another, in order to
catch prisoners. By such wicked and inhuman ways the English are
said to enslave towards one hundred thousand yearly; of which thirty
thousand are supposed to die by barbarous treatment in the first year;
besides all that are slain in the unnatural wars excited to take them.

---

  *Dr. Ames, Baxter, Durham, Locke, Carmichael, Hutcheson, Montesquieu, and
Blackstone, Wallace, etc., etc. Bishop of Gloucester.—*Author.*
  [What work of Dr. (?William) Ames is referred to I have not found. The others are
Baxter's "Christian Directory"; James Durham's "Law Unsealed"; John Locke's "Of Gov-
ernment"; Gerschomus Carmichael's "Puffendorf"; Francis Hutcheson's "System of
Moral Philosophy"; Montesquieu's "Spirit of the Laws"; Blackstone's "Commentaries";
Dr. George Wallace on the ancient peerages of Scotland; "Sermon before the Society for
the Propagation of the Gospel, 21 February 1766," by the Bishop of Gloucester (War-
burton).—*Editor.*] [Note: All references to "Editor" are to Moncure Daniel Conway, the
nineteenth-century editor of Thomas Paine's writings.]

So much innocent blood have the Managers and Supporters of this inhuman Trade to answer for to the common Lord of all!

Many of these were not prisoners of war, and redeemed from savage conquerors, as some plead; and they who were such prisoners, the English, who promote the war for that very end, are the guilty authors of their being so; and if they were redeemed, as is alleged, they would owe nothing to the redeemer but what he paid for them.

They show as little Reason as Conscience who put the matter by with saying—"Men, in some cases, are lawfully made Slaves, and why may not these?" So men, in some cases, are lawfully put to death, deprived of their goods, without their consent; may any man, therefore, be treated so, without any conviction of desert? Nor is this plea mended by adding—"They are set forth to us as slaves, and we buy them without farther inquiry, let the sellers see to it." Such men may as well join with a known band of robbers, buy their ill-got goods, and help on the trade; ignorance is no more pleadable in one case than the other; the sellers plainly own how they obtain them. But none can lawfully buy without evidence that they are not concurring with Men-Stealers; and as the true owner has a right to reclaim his goods that were stolen, and sold; so the slave, who is proper owner of his freedom, has a right to reclaim it, however often sold.

Most shocking of all is alledging the Sacred Scriptures to favour this wicked practice. One would have thought none but infidel cavillers would endeavour to make them appear contrary to the plain dictates of natural light, and Conscience, in a matter of common Justice and Humanity; which they cannot be. Such worthy men, as referred to before, judged otherways; MR. BAXTER declared, *the Slave-Traders should be called Devils, rather than Christians; and that it is a heinous crime to buy them.* But some say, "the practice was permitted to the Jews." To which may be replied,

1. The example of the Jews may not be imitated by us; they had not only orders to cut off several nations altogether, but if they were obliged to war with others, and conquered them, to cut off every male; they were suffered to use polygamy and divorces, and other things utterly unlawful to us under clearer light.

2. The plea is, in a great measure, false; they had no permission to catch and enslave people who never injured them.

3. Such arguments ill become us, *since the time of reformation came,* under Gospel light. All distinctions of nations, and privileges of one above others, are ceased; Christians are taught to *account all men their*

neighbours; and love their neighbours as themselves; and do to all men as they would be done by; to do good to all men; and Man-stealing is ranked with enormous crimes. Is the barbarous enslaving our inoffensive neighbours, and treating them like wild beasts subdued by force, reconcilable with all these *Divine precepts?* Is this doing to them as we would desire they should do to us? If they could carry off and enslave some thousands of us, would we think it just?—One would almost wish they could for once; it might convince more than Reason, or the Bible.

As much in vain, perhaps, will they search ancient history for examples of the modern Slave-Trade. Too many nations enslaved the prisoners they took in war. But to go to nations with whom there is no war, who have no way provoked, without farther design of conquest, purely to catch inoffensive people, like wild beasts, for slaves, is an hight of outrage against Humanity and Justice, that seems left by Heathen nations to be practised by pretended Christians. How shameful are all attempts to colour and excuse it!

As these people are not convicted of forfeiting freedom, they have still a natural, perfect right to it; and the Governments whenever they come should, in justice set them free, and punish those who hold them in slavery.

So monstrous is the making and keeping them slaves at all, abstracted from the barbarous usage they suffer, and the many evils attending the practice; as selling husbands away from wives, children from parents, and from each other, in violation of sacred and natural ties; and opening the way for adulteries, incests, and many shocking consequences, for all of which the guilty Masters must answer to the final judge.

If the slavery of the parents be unjust, much more is their children's; if the parents were justly slaves, yet the children are born free; this is the natural, perfect right of all mankind; they are nothing but a just recompense to those who bring them up: And as much less is commonly spent on them than others, they have a right, in justice, to be proportionably sooner free.

Certainly one may, with as much reason and decency, plead for murder, robbery, lewdness, and barbarity, as for this practice: They are not more contrary to the natural dictates of Conscience, and feelings of Humanity; nay, they are all comprehended in it.

But the chief design of this paper is not to disprove it, which many have sufficiently done; but to entreat Americans to consider

1. With what consistency, or decency they complain so loudly of attempts to enslave them, while they hold so many hundred thousands

in slavery; and annually enslave many thousands more, without any pretence of authority, or claim upon them?

2. How just, how suitable to our crime is the punishment with which Providence threatens us? We have enslaved multitudes, and shed much innocent blood in doing it; and now are threatened with the same. And while other evils are confessed, and bewailed, why not this especially, and publicly; than which no other vice, if all others, has brought so much guilt on the land?

3. Whether, then, all ought not immediately to discontinue and renounce it, with grief and abhorrence? Should not every society bear testimony against it, and account obstinate persisters in it bad men, enemies to their country, and exclude them from fellowship; as they often do for much lesser faults?

4. The great Question may be—What should be done with those who are enslaved already? To turn the old and infirm free, would be injustice and cruelty; they who enjoyed the labours of their better days should keep, and treat them humanely. As to the rest, let prudent men, with the assistance of legislatures, determine what is practicable for masters, and best for them. Perhaps some could give them lands upon reasonable rent, some, employing them in their labour still, might give them some reasonable allowances for it; so as all may have some property, and fruits of their labours at their own disposal, and be encouraged to industry; the family may live together, and enjoy the natural satisfaction of exercising relative affections and duties, with civil protection, and other advantages, like fellow men. Perhaps they might sometime form useful barrier settlements on the frontiers. Thus they may become interested in the public welfare, and assist in promoting it; instead of being dangerous, as now they are, should any enemy promise them a better condition.

5. The past treatment of Africans must naturally fill them with abhorrence of Christians; lead them to think our religion would make them more inhuman savages, if they embraced it; thus the gain of that trade has been pursued in opposition to the Redeemer's cause, and the happiness of men: Are we not, therefore, bound in duty to him and to them to repair these injuries, as far as possible, by taking some proper measures to instruct, not only the slaves here, but the Africans in their own countries? Primitive Christians laboured always to spread their *Divine Religion;* and this is equally our duty while there is an Heathen nation: But what singular obligations are we under to these injured people!

These are the sentiments of

JUSTICE AND HUMANITY.

2

A Serious Thought

October 18, 1775

This short essay, which appeared in the Pennsylvania Journal *on October 18, 1775, is remarkable for the way in which it links slavery to the cause of independence from Great Britain.* "A Serious Thought" appeared just three months before* Common Sense, *Paine's ringing call to arms. Even more remarkably, "A Serious Thought" anticipated the logic of Thomas Jefferson, who listed the slave trade among American grievances against Great Britain in his draft of the Declaration of Independence.*

The most famous and longest passage of Jefferson's draft excised by Congress blamed King George III for the institution of slavery. Ever since, historians have recognized Jefferson's argument as hyperbolic, a blatant distortion of history for the purposes of vilifying the king and rationalizing Jefferson's continued ownership of slaves. It seems clear, though, that when Jefferson accused George III of waging "cruel war against human nature itself," he was pursuing a line of logic developed by Paine a year earlier. "A Serious Thought" is Paine's telling of the same history.

When I reflect on the horrid cruelties exercised by Britain in the East Indies—How thousands perished by artificial famine—How religion and every manly principle of honour and honesty were sacrificed to luxury and pride—When I read of the wretched natives being blown away, for no other crime than because, sickened with the miserable scene, they refused to fight—When I reflect on these and a thousand instances of similar barbarity, I firmly believe that the Almighty, in compassion to mankind, will curtail the power of Britain.

And when I reflect on the use she hath made of the discovery of this new world—that the little paltry dignity of earthly kings hath been set up in preference to the great cause of the King of kings— That instead of Christian examples to the Indians, she hath basely

---

Pennsylvania Journal, October 18, 1775. This was probably the earliest anticipation of the Declaration of Independence written and published in America.—*Editor.*

Moncure Daniel Conway, *The Writings of Thomas Paine,* 2 vols. (New York: G. P. Putnam's Sons, 1894): 1, 65–66.

tampered with their passions, imposed on their ignorance, and made them tools of treachery and murder—And when to these and many other melancholy reflections I add this sad remark, that ever since the discovery of America she hath employed herself in the most horrid of all traffics, that of human flesh, unknown to the most savage nations, hath yearly (without provocation and in cold blood) ravaged the hapless shores of Africa, robbing it of its unoffending inhabitants to cultivate her stolen dominions in the West—When I reflect on these, I hesitate not for a moment to believe that the Almighty will finally separate America from Britain. Call it Independence or what you will, if it is the cause of God and humanity it will go on.

And when the Almighty shall have blest us, and made us a people *dependent only upon Him,* then may our first gratitude be shown by an act of continental legislation, which shall put a stop to the importation of Negroes for sale, soften the hard fate of those already here, and in time procure their freedom.

HUMANUS.

3

A Dialogue between General Wolfe and General Gage in a Wood Near Boston[1]

January 4, 1775

This essay was the first one published, although not the first written by Paine after his arrival in America. It appeared in the January 4, 1775, issue of the Pennsylvania Journal. *It shows Paine using the literary device of an imaginary dialogue, a technique that he would return to several times in his writings. Here we also see Paine comparing humans contemptuously to animals, in this case a "war horse" and an "elephant." We will see this again in* Common Sense, *where Paine describes the British monarch as a "royal brute" and where humans are compared to a "herd of common animals," as well as to worms. When the ghost of General Wolfe*

---

[1]From the *Pennsylvania Journal,* January 4, 1775.

Moncure Daniel Conway, *The Writings of Thomas Paine,* 2 vols. (New York: G. P. Putnam's Sons, 1894): 1, 10–13.

calls for courage and a patriotic resistance to tyranny, he uses imagery that American readers would have recognized from the English Civil War and the Glorious Revolution of the seventeenth century. When Englishmen executed Charles I and insisted on the contractual nature of government, they left a legacy of rights that Paine now called on Americans to defend. These were times, Wolfe tells Gage and Paine reminds Americans, when again resistance to a monarch was not only justified, but essential.

Gen. Wolfe: Welcome my old friend to this retreat.

Gen. Gage: I am glad to see you my dear Mr. Wolfe, but what has brought you back again to this world?

Gen. Wolfe: I am sent by a group of British heroes to remonstrate with you upon your errand to this place. You are come upon a business unworthy a British soldier, and a freeman. You have come here to deprive your fellow subjects of their liberty.

Gen. Gage: God forbid! I am come here to execute the orders of my Sovereign,—a Prince of unbounded wisdom and goodness, and who aims at no higher honor than that of being the King of a free people.

Gen. Wolfe: Strange language from a British soldier! I honour the crown of Great-Britain as an essential part of her excellent constitution. I served a Sovereign to whom the impartial voice of posterity has ascribed the justice of the man as well as the magnanimity of a King, and yet such was the free spirit of the troops under my command, that I could never animate them with a proper martial spirit without setting before them the glorious objects, of their King and their COUNTRY.

Gen. Gage: The orders of my Sovereign have been sanctified by the Parliament of Great-Britain. All the wisdom and liberty of the whole empire are collected in that august Assembly. My troops therefore cannot want the same glorious motives which animated yours, in the present expedition. They will fight for their country as well as their King.

Gen. Wolfe: The wisest assemblies of men are as liable as individuals, to corruption and error. The greatest ravages which have ever been committed upon the liberty and happiness of mankind have been by weak and corrupted republics. The American colonies are entitled to all the privileges of British subjects. Equality of liberty is the glory of every Briton. He does not forfeit it by crossing the Ocean. He carries it with him into the most distant parts of the world, because he carries with him the immutable laws of nature. A Briton or an American ceases to be a British subject when he ceases to be governed by rulers chosen or approved of by himself. This is the essence of liberty and of the British constitution.

Gen. Gage: The inhabitants of the province of Massachusetts Bay have not only thrown off the jurisdiction of the British Parliament, but they are disaffected to the British crown. They cannot even bear with that small share of regal power and grandeur which have been delegated to the Governors of this province. They traduced Sir Francis Bernard, and petitioned the King to remove Mr. Hutchinson from the seat of government. But their opposition to my administration has arisen to open rebellion. They have refused to obey my proclamations. They have assembled and entered into associations to eat no mutton and to wear clothes manufactured in this country,—they have even provided themselves with arms and ammunition, and have acquired a complete knowledge of the military exercises, in direct opposition to my proclamations.

Gen. Wolfe: The inhabitants of Massachusetts Bay were once a brave and *loyal* people. If they are disaffected to his present Majesty, it is because his Ministers have sent counterfeit impressions of his royal virtues to govern them. Bernard and Hutchinson must have been a composition of all the base and wicked qualities in human nature to have diminished the loyalty of those illustrious subjects, or weakened their devotion to every part of the British constitution.—I must add here that the late proceedings of the British Parliament towards the American colonists have reached the British heroes in Elysium, and have produced a suspension of their happiness. The Quebec Bill in a particular manner has roused their resentment. It was once the glory of Englishmen to draw the sword only in defence of liberty and the protestant religion, or to extend the blessings of both to their unhappy neighbours. These godlike motives reconciled me to all the hardships of that campaign which ended in the reduction of Canada. These godlike motives likewise reconciled me to the horror I felt in being obliged to shed the blood of those brave Frenchmen, who opposed me on the plains of Abraham. I rejoiced less in the hour of my death, in the honor of my victory, than in the glory of having communicated to an inslaved people the glorious privileges of an English constitution. While my fellow soldiers hailed me as their conqueror, I exulted only in being their DELIVERER. But popery and French laws in Canada are but a part of that system of despotism, which has been prepared for the colonies. The edicts of the British Parliament (for they want the sanction of British laws) which relate to the province of Massachusetts Bay are big with destruction to the whole British empire. I come therefore in the name of Blakeney—Cumberland—Granby—and an illustrious band of English heroes to whom the glory of Old England is still dear, to beg you to have no hand in the execution of them. Remember Sir you are a man as well as a soldier. You did not give up your privileges as a citizen when you put on your sword. British soldiers are not machines, to be animated only with the voice of a Minister of State. They disdain those ideas of submission which preclude them from the liberty of thinking for themselves, and degrade them to an equality with a war horse, or an elephant. If you value the sweets of peace and liberty,—if you have any regard to the glory of the British name, and if you prefer the society of Grecian, Roman, and British heroes in the world of spirits, to the company of Jeffries, Kirk, and other royal executioners, I conjure you immediately to resign your commission. Assign the above reasons to your Sovereign for your conduct, and you will have the *sole* glory of performing an action which would do honour to an angel. You will restore perpetual harmony between Britain and her colonies.

4

*Thoughts on Defensive War**

July 1775

This essay, published in the Pennsylvania Magazine *during July 1775, reveals a number of themes and devices that Paine draws on again for* Common Sense. *The title, the signature ("A Lover of Peace"), and the logic of the essay itself are deeply rooted in Paine's Quaker upbringing. There are a number of direct references to Quaker beliefs. Paine attempts to reconcile his belief that war is sometimes necessary with the Quakers' Peace Testimony, which led many Quakers to be pacifists. Paine also selectively uses the Bible to support his argument, as he does again in* Common Sense. *The vitriolic language of this essay—"unprincipled enemy," "Highwayman," "madman of Macedon"—is one of Paine's trademarks. The rationalistic aphorisms—"we live not in a world of angels," "the balance of power is the scale of peace"—show a way of thinking and a form*

---

*From the *Pennsylvania Magazine,* July, 1775. Probably by Paine.—*Editor.*

Moncure Daniel Conway, *The Writings of Thomas Paine,* 2 vols. (New York: G. P. Putnam's Sons, 1894): 1, 55–58.

of expression that are recognizably Paine's. Finally, observe Paine's use of parent and child figures in the essay, which is also a hallmark of Common Sense.

Could the peaceable principle of the Quakers be universally established, arms and the art of war would be wholly extirpated: But we live not in a world of angels. The reign of Satan is not ended; neither are we to expect to be defended by miracles. The pillar of the cloud existed only in the wilderness. In the nonage of the Israelites. It protected them in their retreat from Pharaoh, while they were *destitute* of the natural means of defence, for they brought no arms from Egypt; but it neither fought their battles nor shielded them from dangers afterwards.

I am thus far a Quaker, that I would gladly agree with all the world to lay aside the use of arms, and settle matters by negotiation; but unless the whole will, the matter ends, and I take up my musket and thank heaven he has put it in my power.

Whoever considers the unprincipled enemy we have to cope with, will not hesitate to declare that nothing but arms or miracles can reduce them to reason and moderation. They have lost sight of the limits of humanity. The portrait of a parent red with the blood of her children is a picture fit only for the galleries of the infernals. From the House of Commons the troops of Britain have been exhorted to fight, not for the defence of their natural rights, not to repel the invasion or the insult of enemies; but on the vilest of all pretences, gold. "Ye fight for solid revenue" was vociferated in the House. Thus America *must suffer* because she has something to lose. Her crime is property. That which allures the Highwayman has allured the ministry under a gentler name. But the position laid down by Lord Sandwich, is a clear demonstration of the justice of defensive arms. The Americans, quoth this Quixote of modern days, *will not fight;* therefore we will. His Lordship's plan when analized amounts to this. These people are either too superstitiously religious, or too cowardly for arms; they either *cannot* or *dare not* defend; their property is open to any one who has the courage to attack them. Send but your troops and the prize is ours. Kill a few and take the whole. Thus the peaceable part of mankind will be continually overrun by the vile and abandoned, while they neglect the means of self defence. The supposed quietude of a good man allures the ruffian; while on the other hand, arms like laws discourage and keep the invader and the plunderer in awe, and preserve order in the world as well as property. The balance of power is the scale of peace. The same balance would be preserved were all the world destitute of arms, for all would be alike; but since some *will not,* others *dare not* lay them aside. And while a single nation refuses to lay them down, it is proper that all should keep them up. Horrid mischief would ensue were one half the world deprived of the use of them; for while avarice and ambition have a place in the heart of man, the weak will become a prey to the strong. The history of every age and nation establishes these truths, and facts need but little arguments when they prove themselves.

But there is a point to view this matter in of superior consequence to the defence of property; and that point is *Liberty* in all its meanings. In the barbarous ages of the world, men in general had no liberty. The strong governed the weak at will; 'till the coming of Christ there was no such thing as political freedom in any known part of the earth. The Jewish kings were in point of government as absolute as the Pharaohs. Men were frequently put to death without trial at the will of the Sovereign. The Romans held the world in slavery, and were themselves the slaves of their emperors. The madman of Macedon governed by caprice and passion, and strided as arrogantly over the world as if he had made and peopled it; and it is needless to imagine that other nations at that time were more refined. Wherefore political as well as spiritual freedom is the gift of God through Christ. The second in the catalogue of blessings; and so intimately related, so sympathetically united with the first, that the one cannot be wounded without communicating an injury to the other. Political liberty is the visible pass which guards the religions. It is the outwork by which the church militant is defended, and the attacks of the enemy are frequently made through this fortress. The same power which has established a restraining Port Bill in the Colonies, has established a restraining Protestant Church Bill in Canada.

I had the pleasure and advantage of hearing this matter wisely investigated, by a gentleman, in a sermon to one of the battalions of this city; and am fully convinced, that spiritual freedom is the root of political liberty.

First. Because till spiritual freedom was made manifest, political liberty did not exist.

Secondly. Because in proportion that *spiritual freedom* has been manifested, *political liberty* has encreased.

Thirdly. Whenever the visible church has been oppressed, political freedom has suffered with it. Read the history of Mary and the Stuarts. The popish world at this day by not knowing the full manifestation of spiritual freedom, enjoy but a shadow of political liberty.—Though I am unwilling to accuse the present government of popish principles, they cannot, I think, be clearly acquitted of popish practices; the facility with which they perceive the dark and ignorant are governed, in popish nations, will always be a temptation to the lovers of arbitrary power to adopt the same methods.

As the union between spiritual freedom and political liberty seems nearly inseparable, it is our duty to defend both. And defence in the first instance is best. The lives of hundreds of both countries had been preserved had America been in arms a year ago. Our enemies have mistaken our peace for cowardice, and supposing us unarmed have begun the attack.

A LOVER OF PEACE.

5

Reflections on Unhappy Marriages[*]
June 1775

This essay, which appeared in a June 1775 issue of the Pennsylvania Mag-azine, *is both critical and hopeful. It reflects Paine's general disposition to claim America as an opportunity for himself and others to improve on the European experience. "Reflections" is significant both for its insights to Paine's tortured relationships and for his presumptions about the emotional makeup of other men. Here, in this link between Paine's private life and his public writing, are some clues to the genius that informed Com-mon Sense. "Reflections" shows Paine writing from the gut, rather than the head, as he will continue to do more effectively than any of the American Revolution's other pamphleteers. Never again, however, does Paine publish an essay that addresses his failings with women and matrimony. We will never get closer to Paine's views on his marriages than we get here.*

---

[*]From the *Pennsylvania Magazine,* June, 1775, where it is appended to a series of papers ("The Old Bachelor") which Paine did not write. The writer says he has "tran-scribed" it. — *Editor.*

Moncure Daniel Conway, *The Writings of Thomas Paine,* 2 vols. (New York: G. P. Put-nam's Sons, 1894): 1, 51–54.

Though 't is confessed on all hands that the weal or woe of life depends on no one circumstance so critical as matrimony, yet how few seem to be influenced by this universal acknowledgement, or act with a caution becoming the danger.

Those that are undone this way, are the young, the rash and amorous, whose hearts are ever glowing with desire, whose eyes are ever roaming after beauty; these doat on the first amiable image that chance throws in their way, and when the flame is once kindled, would risk eternity itself to appease it.—But, still like their first parents, they no sooner taste the tempting fruit, but their eyes are opened: the folly of their intemperance becomes visible; shame succeeds first, and then repentance; but sorrow for themselves soon returns to anger with the innocent cause of their unhappiness. Hence flow bitter reproaches, and keen invectives, which end in mutual hatred and contempt: Love abhors clamour and soon flies away, and happiness finds no entrance when love is gone; Thus for a few hours of dalliance, I will not call it affection, the repose of all their future days are sacrificed; and those who but just before seem'd to live only for each other, now would almost cease to live, that the separation might be eternal.

But hold, says the man of phlegm and economy, all are not of this hasty turn—I allow it—there are persons in the world who are young without passions, and in health without appetite: these hunt out a wife as they go to *Smithfield* for a horse; and inter-marry fortunes, not minds, or even bodies: In this case the Bridegroom has no joy but in taking possession of the portion, and the bride dreams of little beside new clothes, visits and congratulations. Thus, as their expectations of pleasure are not very great, neither is the disappointment very grievous; they just keep each other in countenance, live decently, and are exactly as fond the twentieth year of matrimony, as the first. But I would not advise any one to call this state of insipidity happiness, because it would argue him both ignorant of its nature, and incapable of enjoying it. Mere absence of pain will undoubtedly constitute ease; and, without ease, there can be no happiness: Ease, however, is but the medium, through which happiness is tasted, and but passively receives what the last actually bestows; if therefore the rash who marry inconsiderately, perish in the storms raised by their own passions, these slumber away their days in a sluggish calm, and rather dream they live, than experience it by a series of actual sensible enjoyments.

As matrimonial happiness is neither the result of insipidity, or ill-grounded passion, surely those, who make their court to age, ugliness, and all that 's detestable both in mind and body, cannot hope to find it, tho' qualified with all the riches that avarice covets, or *Plutus* could bestow. Matches of this kind are downright prostitution, however softened by the letter of the law; and he or she who receives the golden equivalent of youth and beauty, so wretchedly bestowed, can never enjoy what they so dearly purchased: The shocking incumbrance would render the sumptuous banquet tasteless, and the magnificent bed loathsome; rest would disdain the one, and appetite sicken at the other; uneasiness wait upon both; even gratitude itself would almost cease to be obliging, and good-manners grow such a burden, that the best bred or best-natured people breathing, would be often tempted to throw it down.

But say we should not wonder that those who either marry gold without love, or love without gold, should be miserable: I can't forbear being astonished, if such whose fortunes are affluent, whose desires were mutual, who equally languished for the happy moment before it came, and seemed for a while to be equally transported when it had taken place: If even these should, in the end, prove as unhappy as either of the others! And yet how often is this the melancholy circumstance! As extasy abates, coolness succeeds, which often makes way for indifference, and that for neglect: Sure of each other by the nuptial band, they no longer take any pains to be mutually agreeable; careless if they displease; and yet angry if reproached; with so little relish for each other's company, that anybody's else is welcome, and more entertaining. Their union thus broke, they pursue separate pleasures; never meet but to wrangle, or part but to find comfort in other society. After this the descent is easy to utter aversion, which having wearied itself out with heart-burnings, clamours, and affronts, subsides into a perfect insensibility; when fresh objects of love step in to their relief on either side, and mutual infidelity makes way for mutual complaisance, that each may be the better able to deceive the other.

I shall conclude with the sentiments of an American savage on this subject, who being advised by one of our countrymen to marry according to the ceremonies of the church, as being the ordinance of an infinitely wise and good God, briskly replied, "That either the Christians' God was not so good and wise as he was represented, or he never meddled with the marriages of his people; since not one in a hundred of them had anything to do either with happiness or common sense. Hence," continued he, "as soon as ever you meet you long to part; and, not having this relief in your power, by way of revenge, double each other's misery: Whereas in ours, which have no other ceremony than mutual affection, and last no longer than they bestow mutual pleasures, we make it our business to oblige the heart we are afraid to lose; and being at liberty to separate, seldom or never feel the inclination. But if any should be found so wretched among us, as to hate where the only commerce ought to be love, we instantly dissolve the band: God made us all in pairs; each has his mate somewhere or other; and 't is our duty to find each other out, since no creature was ever intended to be miserable."

6

Common Sense
January 10, 1776

We know that Paine conceived Common Sense *even before he wrote some of the 1775 essays. There are passages, phrases, techniques, beliefs, and ideas in* Common Sense *that parallel those in the earlier essays. The emotion, logic, use of the Bible, parent-child metaphors, Quakerisms, and comparisons of humans to animals are all things that readers of Paine's 1775 essays had seen before. And yet, nothing of Paine's or anyone else's can prepare a reader for the experience of* Common Sense. *It is Paine's best work and hones his style to a fine point that he never really sustained again. We must keep in mind that most Americans heard rather than read* Common Sense *the first time. We must recall that Americans deeply identified with British culture and their English heritage when this pamphlet first appeared in January 1776. We must remember how religious and how patriotic Americans were and try to appreciate how jarring the words of* Common Sense *must have been.*

Some would say in retrospect that the war had begun two years earlier. The Boston Tea Party, the Intolerable Acts, and the Battles of Lexington and Concord were all past. But when the first shots were fired, Pennsylvania's government was dominated by conservatives — a coalition of Quakers, Germans, and commercial interests not at all sympathetic to the pleas of Boston radicals. So, the decision for Revolution was far from reached when Common Sense *appeared.*

Thomas Paine, *Common Sense* (Philadelphia: Benjamin Towne Printing, 1776), 5–59.

Before the publication of Common Sense, *not a single Pennsylvanian had expressed support for independence. Many already believed that George III and his advisors were misguided, if not treacherous, but it took Thomas Paine to convince them that monarchy in general and the British Constitution in particular were useless.* Common Sense *inspired the radical movement in Pennsylvania and very quickly, during February 1776, the radicals seized Paine's ideas and gained the initiative over moderates in the propaganda war that ensued.*

Addressed to the Inhabitants of America

Man knows no Master save creating HEAVEN,
Or those whom Choice and common Good ordain.
—Thomson.[1]

February 14, 1776

INTRODUCTION

Perhaps the sentiments contained in the following pages, are not *yet* sufficiently fashionable to procure them general favor; a long habit of not thinking a thing *wrong,* gives it a superficial appearance of being *right,* and raises at first a formidable outcry in defence of custom. But the tumult soon subsides. Time makes more converts than reason.

As a long and violent abuse of power, is generally the Means of calling the right of it in question (and in Matters too which might never have been thought of, had not the Sufferers been aggravated into the inquiry) and as the King of England hath undertaken in his *own Right,* to support the Parliament in what he calls *Theirs,* and as the good people of this country are grievously oppressed by the combination, they have an undoubted privilege to inquire into the pretensions of both, and equally to reject the usurpation of either.

In the following sheets, the author hath studiously avoided every thing which is personal among ourselves. Compliments as well as censure to individuals make no part thereof. The wise, and the worthy,

---

[1]James Thomson, *Liberty: A Poem* (1736).

need not the triumph of a pamphlet; and those whose sentiments are injudicious, or unfriendly, will cease of themselves unless too much pains are bestowed upon their conversion.

The cause of America is in a great measure the cause of all mankind. Many circumstances hath, and will arise, which are not local, but universal, and through which the principles of all Lovers of Mankind are affected, and in the Event of which, their Affections are interested. The laying a Country desolate with Fire and Sword, declaring War against the natural rights of all Mankind, and extirpating the Defenders thereof from the Face of the Earth, is the Concern of every Man to whom Nature hath given the Power of feeling; of which Class, regardless of Party Censure, is the

AUTHOR.

P. S. The Publication of this new Edition hath been delayed, with a View of taking notice (had it been necessary) of any Attempt to refute the Doctrine of Independance: As no Answer hath yet appeared, it is now presumed that none will, the Time needful for getting such a Performance ready for the Public being considerably past.

Who the Author of this Production is, is wholly unnecessary to the Public, as the Object for Attention is the *Doctrine itself,* not the *Man.* Yet it may not be unnecessary to say, That he is unconnected with any Party, and under no sort of Influence public or private, but the influence of reason and principle.

Philadelphia, February 14, 1776.

COMMON SENSE.

Of the Origin and Design of Government in General. With Concise Remarks on the English Constitution.

Some writers have so confounded society with government, as to leave little or no distinction between them; whereas they are not only different, but have different origins. Society is produced by our wants, and government by our wickedness; the former promotes our happiness *positively* by uniting our affections, the latter *negatively* by restraining our vices. The one encourages intercourse, the other creates distinctions. The first is a patron, the last a punisher.

Society in every state is a blessing, but government even in its best state is but a necessary evil; in its worst state an intolerable one; for when we suffer, or are exposed to the same miseries *by a government,* which we might expect in a country *without government,* our calamity is heightened by reflecting that we furnish the means by which we suffer. Government, like dress, is the badge of lost innocence; the palaces of kings are built on the ruins of the bowers of paradise. For were the impulses of conscience clear, uniform, and irresistably obeyed, man would need no other lawgiver; but that not being the case, he finds it necessary to surrender up a part of his property to furnish means for the protection of the rest; and this he is induced to do by the same prudence which in every other case advises him out of two evils to choose the least. *Wherefore,* security being the true design and end of government, it unanswerably follows that whatever *form* thereof appears most likely to ensure it to us, with the least expence and greatest benefit, is preferable to all others.

In order to gain a clear and just idea of the design and end of government, let us suppose a small number of persons settled in some sequestered part of the earth, unconnected with the rest, they will then represent the first peopling of any country, or of the world. In this state of natural liberty, society will be their first thought. A thousand motives will excite them thereto, the strength of one man is so unequal to his wants, and his mind so unfitted for perpetual solitude, that he is soon obliged to seek assistance and relief of another, who in his turn requires the same. Four or five united would be able to raise a tolerable dwelling in the midst of a wilderness, but *one* man might labour out the common period of life without accomplishing any thing; when he had felled his timber he could not remove it, nor erect it after it was removed; hunger in the mean time would urge him from his work, and every different want call him a different way. Disease, nay even misfortune would be death, for though neither might be mortal, yet either would disable him from living, and reduce him to a state in which he might rather be said to perish than to die.

Thus necessity, like a gravitating power, would soon form our newly arrived emigrants into society, the reciprocal blessings of which, would supersede, and render the obligations of law and government unnecessary while they remained perfectly just to each other; but as nothing but heaven is impregnable to vice, it will unavoidably happen, that in proportion as they surmount the first difficulties of emigration, which bound them together in a common cause, they will begin to relax in their duty and attachment to each other; and this remissness, will point out the necessity, of establishing some form of government to supply the defect of moral virtue.

Some convenient tree will afford them a State-House, under the branches of which, the whole colony may assemble to deliberate on public matters. It is more than probable that their first laws will have the title only of REGULATIONS, and be enforced by no other penalty than public disesteem. In this first parliament every man, by natural right, will have a seat.

But as the colony increases, the public concerns will increase likewise, and the distance at which the members may be separated, will render it too inconvenient for all of them to meet on every occasion as at first, when their number was small, their habitations near, and the public concerns few and trifling. This will point out the convenience of their consenting to leave the legislative part to be managed by a select number chosen from the whole body, who are supposed to have the same concerns at stake which those have who appointed them, and who will act in the same manner as the whole body would act were they present. If the colony continue increasing, it will become necessary to augment the number of the representatives, and that the interest of every part of the colony may be attended to, it will be found best to divide the whole into convenient parts, each part sending its proper number; and that the *elected* might never form to themselves an interest separate from the *electors,* prudence will point out the propriety of having elections often; because as the *elected* might by that means return and mix again with the general body of the *electors* in a few months, their fidelity to the public will be secured by the prudent reflexion of not making a rod for themselves. And as this frequent interchange will establish a common interest with every part of the community, they will mutually and naturally support each other, and on this (not on the unmeaning name of king) depends the *strength of government, and the happiness of the governed.*

Here then is the origin and rise of government; namely, a mode rendered necessary by the inability of moral virtue to govern the world; here too is the design and end of government, viz. freedom and security. And however our eyes may be dazzled with show, or our ears deceived by sound; however prejudice may warp our wills, or interest darken our understanding, the simple voice of nature and of reason will say, it is right.

I draw my idea of the form of government from a principle in nature, which no art can overturn, viz. that the more simple any thing is, the less liable it is to be disordered, and the easier repaired when disordered; and with this maxim in view, I offer a few remarks on the so much boasted constitution of England. That it was noble for the dark and slavish times in which it was erected, is granted. When the world was over run with tyranny the least remove therefrom was a glorious rescue. But that it is imperfect, subject to convulsions, and incapable of producing what it seems to promise, is easily demonstrated.

Absolute governments (tho' the disgrace of human nature) have this advantage with them, that they are simple; if the people suffer, they know the head from which their suffering springs, know likewise the remedy, and are not bewildered by a variety of causes and cures. But the constitution of England is so exceedingly complex, that the nation may suffer for years together without being able to discover in which part the fault lies, some will say in one and some in another, and every political physician will advise a different medicine.

I know it is difficult to get over local or long standing prejudices, yet if we will suffer ourselves to examine the component parts of the English constitution, we shall find them to be the base remains of two ancient tyrannies, compounded with some new republican materials.

First. —The remains of monarchical tyranny in the person of the king.

Secondly. —The remains of aristocratical tyranny in the persons of the peers.

Thirdly. —The new republican materials, in the persons of the commons, on whose virtue depends the freedom of England.

The two first, by being hereditary, are independent of the people; wherefore in a *constitutional sense* they contribute nothing towards the freedom of the state.

To say that the constitution of England is a *union* of three powers reciprocally *checking* each other, is farcical, either the words have no meaning, or they are flat contradictions.

To say that the commons is a check upon the king, presupposes two things.

First. —That the king is not to be trusted without being looked after, or in other words, that a thirst for absolute power is the natural disease of monarchy.

Secondly. —That the commons, by being appointed for that purpose, are either wiser or more worthy of confidence than the crown.

But as the same constitution which gives the commons a power to check the king by withholding the supplies, gives afterwards the king a power to check the commons, by empowering him to reject their other bills; it again supposes that the king is wiser than those whom it has already supposed to be wiser than him. A mere absurdity!

There is something exceedingly ridiculous in the composition of monarchy; it first excludes a man from the means of information, yet empowers him to act in cases where the highest judgment is required. The state of a king shuts him from the world, yet the business of a king requires him to know it thoroughly; wherefore the different parts, by unnaturally opposing and destroying each other, prove the whole character to be absurd and useless.

Some writers have explained the English constitution thus; the king, say they, is one, the people another; the peers are an house in behalf of the king; the commons in behalf of the people; but this hath all the distinctions of an house divided against itself; and though the expressions be pleasantly arranged, yet when examined they appear idle and ambiguous; and it will always happen, that the nicest construction that words are capable of, when applied to the description of some thing which either cannot exist, or is too incomprehensible to be within the compass of description, will be words of sound only, and though they may amuse the ear, they cannot inform the mind, for this explanation includes a previous question, viz. *How came the king by a power which the people are afraid to trust, and always obliged to check?* Such a power could not be the gift of a wise people, neither can any power, *which needs checking,* be from God; yet the provision, which the constitution makes, supposes such a power to exist.

But the provision is unequal to the task; the means either cannot or will not accomplish the end, and the whole affair is a felo de se; for as the greater weight will always carry up the less, and as all the wheels of a machine are put in motion by one, it only remains to know which power in the constitution has the most weight, for that will govern; and though the others, or a part of them, may clog, or, as the phrase is, check the rapidity of its motion, yet so long as they cannot stop it, their endeavors will be ineffectual; the first moving power will at last have its way, and what it wants in speed is supplied by time.

That the crown is this overbearing part in the English constitution needs not be mentioned, and that it derives its whole consequence merely from being the giver of places and pensions is self-evident, wherefore, though we have been wise enough to shut and lock a door against absolute monarchy, we at the same time have been foolish enough to put the crown in possession of the key.

The prejudice of Englishmen, in favour of their own government by king, lords and commons, arises as much or more from national pride than reason. Individuals are undoubtedly safer in England than in some other countries, but the *will* of the king is as much the *law* of the land in Britain as in France, with this difference, that instead of proceeding directly from his mouth, it is handed to the people under the more formidable shape of an act of parliament. For the fate of Charles the first, hath only made kings more subtle—not more just.

Wherefore, laying aside all national pride and prejudice in favour of modes and forms, the plain truth is, that *it is wholly owing to the constitution of the people, and not to the constitution of the government* that the crown is not as oppressive in England as in Turkey.

An inquiry into the *constitutional errors* in the English form of government is at this time highly necessary, for as we are never in a proper condition of doing justice to others, while we continue under the influence of some leading partiality, so neither are we capable of doing it to ourselves while we remain fettered by any obstinate prejudice. And as a man, who is attached to a prostitute, is unfitted to choose or judge of a wife, so any prepossession in favour of a rotten constitution of government will disable us from discerning a good one.

Of Monarchy and Heredity Succession

Mankind being originally equals in the order of creation, the equality could only be destroyed by some subsequent circumstance; the distinctions of rich, and poor, may in a great measure be accounted for, and that without having recourse to the harsh ill sounding names of oppression and avarice. Oppression is often the *consequence,* but seldom or never the *means* of riches; and though avarice will preserve a man from being necessitously poor, it generally makes him too timorous to be wealthy.

But there is another and greater distinction for which no truly natural or religious reason can be assigned, and that is, the distinction of men into KINGS and SUBJECTS. Male and female are the distinctions of nature, good and bad the distinctions of heaven; but how a race of men came into the world so exalted above the rest, and distinguished like some new species, is worth enquiring into, and whether they are the means of happiness or of misery to mankind.

In the early ages of the world, according to the scripture chronology, there were no kings; the consequence of which was there were no wars; it is the pride of kings which throw mankind into confusion. Holland without a king hath enjoyed more peace for this last century than any of the monarchical governments in Europe. Antiquity favors the same remark; for the quiet and rural lives of the first patriarchs hath a happy something in them, which vanishes away when we come to the history of Jewish royalty.

Government by kings was first introduced into the world by the Heathens, from whom the children of Israel copied the custom. It was the most prosperous invention the Devil ever set on foot for the promotion of idolatry. The Heathens paid divine honors to their deceased kings, and the christian world hath improved on the plan by doing the same to their living ones. How impious is the title of sacred majesty applied to a worm, who in the midst of his splendor is crumbling into dust!

As the exalting one man so greatly above the rest cannot be justified on the equal rights of nature, so neither can it be defended on the authority of scripture; for the will of the Almighty, as declared by Gideon and the prophet Samuel, expressly disapproves of government by kings. All anti-monarchical parts of scripture have been very smoothly glossed over in monarchical governments, but they undoubtedly merit the attention of countries which have their governments yet to form. *"Render unto Caesar the things which are Caesar's"* is the scripture doctrine of courts, yet it is no support of monarchical government, for the Jews at that time were without a king, and in a state of vassalage to the Romans.

Near three thousand years passed away from the Mosaic account of the creation, till the Jews under a national delusion requested a king. Till then their form of government (except in extraordinary cases, where the Almighty interposed) was a kind of republic administred by a judge and the elders of the tribes. Kings they had none, and it was held sinful to acknowledge any being under that title but the Lord of Hosts. And when a man seriously reflects on the idolatrous homage which is paid to the persons of Kings, he need not wonder, that the Almighty ever jealous of his honor, should disapprove of a form of government which so impiously invades the prerogative of heaven.

Monarchy is ranked in scripture as one of the sins of the Jews, for which a curse in reserve is denounced against them. The history of that transaction is worth attending to.

The children of Israel being oppressed by the Midianites, Gideon marched against them with a small army, and victory, thro' the divine interposition, decided in his favour. The Jews elate with success, and attributing it to the generalship of Gideon, proposed making him a king, saying, *Rule thou over us, thou and thy son and thy son's son.* Here was temptation in its fullest extent; not a kingdom only, but an hereditary one, but Gideon in the piety of his soul replied, *I will not rule over you, neither shall my son rule over you.* THE LORD SHALL RULE OVER YOU. Words need not be more explicit; Gideon doth not *decline* the honor, but denieth their right to give it; neither doth he compliment them with invented declarations of his thanks, but in the positive stile of a prophet charges them with disaffection to their proper Sovereign, the King of heaven.

About one hundred and thirty years after this, they fell again into the same error. The hankering which the Jews had for the idolatrous customs of the Heathens, is something exceedingly unaccountable; but so it was, that laying hold of the misconduct of Samuel's two sons, who were entrusted with some secular concerns, they came in an abrupt and clamorous manner to Samuel, saying, *Behold thou art old, and thy sons walk not in thy ways, now make us a king to judge us like all the other nations.* And here we cannot but observe that their motives were bad, viz. that they might be *like* unto other nations, i. e. the Heathens, whereas their true glory laid in being as much *unlike* them as possible. *But the thing displeased Samuel when they said, Give us a king to judge us; and Samuel prayed unto the Lord, and the Lord said unto Samuel, Hearken unto the voice of the people in all that they say unto thee, for they have not rejected thee, but they have rejected me,* THAT I SHOULD NOT REIGN OVER THEM. *According to all the works which they have done since the day that I brought them up out of Egypt, even unto this day; wherewith they have forsaken me and served other Gods; so do they also unto thee. Now therefore hearken unto their voice, howbeit, protest solemnly unto them and shew them the manner of the king that shall reign over them, i. e.* not of any particular king, but the general manner of the kings of the earth, whom Israel was so eagerly copying after. And notwithstanding the great distance of time and difference of manners, the character is still in fashion. *And Samuel told all the words of the Lord unto the people, that asked of him a king. And he said, This shall be the manner of the king that shall reign over you; he will take your sons and appoint them for himself, for his chariots, and to be his horsemen, and some shall run before his chariots* (this description agrees with the present mode of impressing men) *and he will appoint him captains over thousands and captains over fifties, and will set them to ear his ground and to reap his harvest, and to make his instruments of war, and instruments of his chariots; and he will take your daughters to be confectionaries, and to be cooks and to be bakers* (this describes the expence and luxury as well as the oppression of kings) *and he will take your fields and your olive yards, even the best of them, and give them to his servants; and he will take the tenth of your feed, and of your vineyards, and give them to his officers and to his servants* (by which we see that bribery, corruption and favoritism are the standing vices of kings) *and he will take the tenth of your men servants, and your maid servants, and your goodliest young men and your asses, and put them to his work; and he will take the tenth of your sheep, and ye shall be his servants, and ye shall cry out in that day because of your king which ye shall have chosen,* AND THE LORD WILL NOT HEAR YOU IN THAT DAY. This accounts for the continuation of monarchy; neither do the characters of the few good kings which have lived since, either sanctify the title, or blot out the sinfulness of the origin; the high encomium given of David takes no notice of him *officially as a king,* but only as a *man* after God's own heart. *Nevertheless the People refused to obey the voice of Samuel, and they said, Nay, but we will have a king over us, that we may be like all the nations, and that our king may judge us, and go out before us, and fight our battles.* Samuel continued to reason with them, but to no purpose; he set before them their ingratitude, but all would not avail; and seeing them fully bent on their folly, he cried out, *I will call unto the Lord, and he shall send thunder and rain* (which then was a punishment, being in the time of wheat harvest) *that ye may perceive and see that your wickedness is great which ye have done in the sight of the Lord,* IN ASKING YOU A KING. *So Samuel called unto the Lord, and the Lord sent thunder and rain that day, and all the people greatly feared the Lord and Samuel. And all the people said unto Samuel, Pray for thy servants unto the Lord thy God that we die not, for* WE HAVE ADDED UNTO OUR SINS THIS EVIL, TO ASK A KING. These portions of scripture are direct and positive. They admit of no equivocal construction. That the Almighty hath here entered his protest against monarchical government is true, or the scripture is false. And a man hath good reason to believe that there is as much of king-craft, as priest-craft, in withholding the scripture from the public in Popish countries. For monarchy in every instance is the Popery of government.

To the evil of monarchy we have added that of hereditary succession; and as the first is a degradation and lessening of ourselves, so the second, claimed as a matter of right, is an insult and an imposition on posterity. For all men being originally equals, no *one* by *birth* could have a right to set up his own family in perpetual preference to all others for ever, and though himself might deserve *some* decent degree of honors of his cotemporaries, yet his descendants might be far too unworthy to inherit them. One of the strongest *natural* proofs of the folly of hereditary right in kings, is, that nature disapproves it, otherwise she would not so frequently turn it into ridicule by giving mankind an *ass for a lion.*

Secondly, as no man at first could possess any other public honors than were bestowed upon him, so the givers of those honors could have no power to give away the right of posterity, and though they might say "We choose you for *our* head," they could not, without manifest injustice to their children say "that your children and your childrens children shall reign over *ours* for ever." Because such an unwise, unjust, unnatural compact might (perhaps) in the next succession put them under the government of a rogue or a fool. Most wise men, in their private sentiments, have ever treated hereditary right with contempt; yet it is one of those evils, which when once established is not easily removed; many submit from fear, others from superstition, and the more powerful part shares with the king the plunder of the rest.

This is supposing the present race of kings in the world to have had an honorable origin; whereas it is more than probable, that could we take off the dark covering of antiquity, and trace them to their first rise, that we should find the first of them nothing better than the principal ruffian of some restless gang, whose savage manners or preeminence in subtility obtained him the title of chief among plunderers; and who by increasing in power, and extending his depredations, overawed the quiet and defenceless to purchase their safety by frequent contributions. Yet his electors could have no idea of giving hereditary right to his descendants, because such a perpetual exclusion of themselves was incompatible with the free and unrestrained principles they professed to live by. Wherefore, hereditary succession in the early ages of monarchy could not take place as a matter of claim, but as something casual or complimental; but as few or no records were extant in those days, and traditionary history stuffed with fables, it was very easy, after the lapse of a few generations, to trump up some superstitious tale, conveniently timed, Mahomet like, to cram hereditary right down the throats of the vulgar. Perhaps the disorders which threatened, or seemed to threaten, on the decease of a leader and the choice of a new one (for elections among ruffians could not be very orderly) induced many at first to favor hereditary pretensions; by which means it happened, as it hath happened since, that what at first was submitted to as a convenience, was afterwards claimed as a right.

England, since the conquest, hath known some few good monarchs, but groaned beneath a much larger number of bad ones; yet no man in his senses can say that their claim under William the Conqueror is a very honorable one. A French bastard landing with an armed banditti, and establishing himself king of England against the consent of the natives, is in plain terms a very paltry rascally original.—It certainly hath no divinity in it. However, it is needless to spend much time in exposing the folly of hereditary right, if there are any so weak as to believe it, let them promiscuously worship the ass and lion, and welcome. I shall neither copy their humility, nor disturb their devotion.

Yet I should be glad to ask how they suppose kings came at first? The question admits but of three answers, viz. either by lot, by election, or by usurpation. If the first king was taken by lot, it establishes a precedent for the next, which excludes hereditary succession. Saul was by lot, yet the succession was not hereditary, neither does it appear from that transaction there was any intention it ever should. If the first king of any country was by election, that likewise establishes a precedent for the next; for to say, that the *right* of all future generations is taken away, by the act of the first electors, in their choice not only of a king, but of a family of kings for ever, hath no parrallel in or out of scripture but the doctrine of original sin, which supposes the free will of all men lost in Adam; and from such comparison, and it will admit of no other, hereditary succession can derive no glory. For as in Adam all sinned, and as in the first electors all men obeyed; as in the one all mankind were subjected to Satan, and in the other to Sovereignty; as our innocence was lost in the first, and our authority in the last; and as both disable us from reassuming some former state and privilege, it unanswerably follows that original sin and hereditary succession are parellels. Dishonorable rank! Inglorious connexion! Yet the most subtile sophist cannot produce a juster simile.

As to usurpation, no man will be so hardy as to defend it; and that William the Conqueror was an usurper is a fact not to be contradicted. The plain truth is, that the antiquity of English monarchy will not bear looking into.

But it is not so much the absurdity as the evil of hereditary succession which concerns mankind. Did it ensure a race of good and wise men it would have the seal of divine authority, but as it opens a door to the *foolish,* the *wicked,* and the *improper,* it hath in it the nature of oppression. Men who look upon themselves born to reign, and others to obey, soon grow insolent; selected from the rest of mankind their minds are early poisoned by importance; and the world they act in differs so materially from the world at large, that they have but little opportunity of knowing its true interests, and when they succeed to the government are frequently the most ignorant and unfit of any throughout the dominions.

Another evil which attends hereditary succession is, that the throne is subject to be possessed by a minor at any age; all which time the regency, acting under the cover of a king, have every opportunity and inducement to betray their trust. The same national misfortune happens, when a king worn out with age and infirmity, enters the last stage of human weakness. In both these cases the public becomes a prey to every miscreant, who can tamper successfully with the follies either of age or infancy.

The most plausible plea, which hath ever been offered in favour of hereditary succession, is, that it preserves a nation from civil wars; and were this true, it would be weighty; whereas, it is the most barefaced falsity ever imposed upon mankind. The whole history of England disowns the fact. Thirty kings and two minors have reigned in that distracted kingdom since the conquest, in which time there have been (including the Revolution) no less than eight civil wars and nineteen rebellions. Wherefore instead of making for peace, it makes against it, and destroys the very foundation it seems to stand on.

The contest for monarchy and succession, between the houses of York and Lancaster, laid England in a scene of blood for many years. Twelve pitched battles, besides skirmishes and sieges, were fought between Henry and Edward. Twice was Henry prisoner to Edward, who in his turn was prisoner to Henry. And so uncertain is the fate of war and the temper of a nation, when nothing but personal matters are the ground of a quarrel, that Henry was taken in triumph from a prison to a palace, and Edward obliged to fly from a palace to a foreign land; yet, as sudden transitions of temper are seldom lasting, Henry in his turn was driven from the throne, and Edward recalled to succeed him. The parliament always following the strongest side.

This contest began in the reign of Henry the Sixth, and was not entirely extinguished till Henry the Seventh, in whom the families were united. Including a period of 67 years, viz. from 1422 to 1489.

In short, monarchy and succession have laid (not this or that kingdom only) but the world in blood and ashes. 'Tis a form of government which the word of God bears testimony against, and blood will attend it.

If we inquire into the business of a king, we shall find that in some countries they have none; and after sauntering away their lives without pleasure to themselves or advantage to the nation, withdraw from the scene, and leave their successors to tread the same idle round. In absolute monarchies the whole weight of business, civil and military, lies on the king; the children of Israel in their request for a king, urged this plea "that he may judge us, and go out before us and fight our battles." But in countries where he is neither a judge nor a general, as in England, a man would be puzzled to know what *is* his business.

The nearer any government approaches to a republic the less business there is for a king. It is somewhat difficult to find a proper name for the government of England. Sir William Meredith calls it a republic; but in its present state it is unworthy of the name, because the corrupt influence of the crown, by having all the places in its disposal, hath so effectually swallowed up the power, and eaten out the virtue of the house of commons (the republican part in the constitution) that the government of England is nearly as monarchical as that of France or Spain. Men fall out with names without understanding them. For it is the republican and not the monarchical part of the constitution of England which Englishmen glory in, viz. the liberty of choosing an house of commons from out of their own body—and it is easy to see that when republican virtue fails, slavery ensues. Why is the constitution of England sickly, but because monarchy hath poisoned the republic, the crown hath engrossed the commons?

In England a king hath little more to do than to make war and give away places; which in plain terms, is to impoverish the nation and set it together by the ears. A pretty business indeed for a man to be allowed eight hundred thousand sterling a year for, and worshipped into the bargain! Of more worth is one honest man to society and in the sight of God, than all the crowned ruffians that ever lived.

Thoughts on the Present State of American Affairs.

In the following pages I offer nothing more than simple facts, plain arguments, and common sense; and have no other preliminaries to settle with the reader, than that he will divest himself of prejudice and prepossession, and suffer his reason and his feelings to determine for themselves; that he will put *on,* or rather that he will not put *off,* the true character of a man, and generously enlarge his views beyond the present day.

Volumes have been written on the subject of the struggle between England and America. Men of all ranks have embarked in the controversy, from different motives, and with various designs; but all have been ineffectual, and the period of debate is closed. Arms, as the last resource, decide the contest; the appeal was the choice of the king, and the continent hath accepted the challenge.

It hath been reported of the late Mr. Pelham (who tho' an able minister was not without his faults) that on his being attacked in the house of commons, on the score, that his measures were only of a temporary kind, replied *"they will last my time."* Should a thought so fatal and unmanly possess the colonies in the present contest, the name of ancestors will be remembered by future generations with detestation.

The sun never shined on a cause of greater worth. 'Tis not the affair of a city, a country, a province, or a kingdom, but of a continent—of at least one eighth part of the habitable globe. 'Tis not the concern of a day, a year, or an age; posterity are virtually involved in the contest, and will be more or less affected, even to the end of time, by the proceedings now. Now is the seed time of continental union, faith and honor. The least fracture now will be like a name engraved with the point of a pin on the tender rind of a young oak; the wound will enlarge with the tree, and posterity read it in full grown characters.

By referring the matter from argument to arms, a new aera for politics is struck; a new method of thinking hath arisen. All plans, proposals, &c. prior to the nineteenth of April,[2] i. e. to the commencement of hostilities, are like the almanacks of the last year; which, though proper then, are superceded and useless now. Whatever was advanced by the advocates on either side of the question then, terminated in one and the same point, viz. a union with Great-Britain; the only difference between the parties was the method of effecting it; the one proposing force, the other friendship; but it hath so far happened that the first hath failed, and the second hath withdrawn her influence.

As much hath been said of the advantages of reconciliation, which, like an agreeable dream, hath passed away and left us as we were, it is but right, that we should examine the contrary side of the argument, and inquire into some of the many material injuries which these colonies sustain, and always will sustain, by being connected with, and dependant on Great-Britain. To examine that connexion and dependance, on the principles of nature and common sense, to see what we have to trust to, if separated, and what we are to expect, if dependant.

I have heard it asserted by some, that as America hath flourished under her former connexion with Great-Britain, that the same connexion is necessary towards her future happiness, and will always have the same effect. Nothing can be more fallacious than this kind of argument. We may as well assert that because a child has thrived upon milk, that it is never to have meat, or that the first twenty years of our lives is to become a precedent for the next twenty. But even this is admitting more than is true, for I answer roundly, that America would have flourished as much, and probably much more, had no European power had any thing to do with her. The commerce, by which she hath enriched herself are the necessaries of life, and will always have a market while eating is the custom of Europe.

But she has protected us, say some. That she hath engrossed us is true, and defended the continent at our expence as well as her own is

[2]Battle of Lexington and Concord.

admitted, and she would have defended Turkey from the same motive, viz. the sake of trade and dominion.

Alas, we have been long led away by ancient prejudices, and made large sacrifices to superstition. We have boasted the protection of Great-Britain, without considering, that her motive was *interest* not *attachment;* that she had did not protect us from *our enemies* on *our account,* but from *her enemies* on *her own account,* from those who had no quarrel with us on any *other account,* and who will always be our enemies on the *same account.* Let Britain wave her pretensions to the continent, or the continent throw off the dependance, and we should be at peace with France and Spain were they at war with Britain. The miseries of Hanover[3] last war ought to warn us against connexions.

It hath lately been asserted in parliament, that the colonies have no relation to each other but through the parent country, *i.e.* that Pennsylvania and the Jerseys, and so on for the rest, are sister colonies by the way of England; this is certainly a very round-about way of proving relationship, but it is the nearest and only true way of proving enemyship, if I may so call it. France and Spain never were, nor perhaps ever will be our enemies as *Americans,* but as our being the *subjects of Great-Britain.*

But Britain is the parent country, say some. Then the more shame upon her conduct. Even brutes do not devour their young, nor savages make war upon their families; wherefore the assertion, if true, turns to her reproach; but it happens not to be true, or only partly so, and the phrase *parent* or *mother country* hath been jesuitically adopted by the king and his parasites, with a low papistical design of gaining an unfair bias on the credulous weakness of our minds. Europe, and not England, is the parent country of America. This new world hath been the asylum for the persecuted lovers of civil and religious liberty from *every part* of Europe. Hither have they fled, not from the tender embraces of the mother, but from the cruelty of the monster; and it is so far true of England, that the same tyranny which drove the first emigrants from home, pursues their descendants still.

In this extensive quarter of the globe, we forget the narrow limits of three hundred and sixty miles (the extent of England) and carry our friendship on a larger scale; we claim brotherhood with every European christian, and triumph in the generosity of the sentiment.

It is pleasant to observe by what regular gradations we surmount the force of local prejudice, as we enlarge our acquaintance with the

---

[3]The German electorate of Hanover, whose ruling dynasty also reigned in Great Britain since 1714, was invaded by the French during the Seven Years War (1754–1763).

world. A man born in any town in England divided into parishes, will naturally associate most with his fellow parishioners (because their interests in many cases will be common) and distinguish him by the name of *neighbour;* if he meet him but a few miles from home, he drops the narrow idea of a street, and salutes him by the name of *townsman;* if he travel out of the county, and meet him in any other, he forgets the minor divisions of street and town, and calls him *country-man,* i.e. *county-man;* but if in their foreign excursions they should associate in France or any other part of *Europe,* their local remembrance would be enlarged into that of *Englishmen.* And by a just parity of reasoning, all Europeans meeting in America, or any other quarter of the globe, are *countrymen;* for England, Holland, Germany, or Sweden, when compared with the whole, stand in the same places on the larger scale, which the divisions of street, town, and county do on the smaller ones; distinctions too limited for continental minds. Not one third of the inhabitants, even of this province, are of English descent. Wherefore I reprobate the phrase of parent or mother country applied to England only, as being false, selfish, narrow and ungenerous.

But admitting, that we were all of English descent, what does it amount to? Nothing. Britain, being now an open enemy, extinguishes every other name and title: And to say that reconciliation is our duty, is truly farcical. The first king of England, of the present line (William the Conqueror) was a Frenchman, and half the Peers of England are descendants from the same country; wherefore, by the same method of reasoning, England ought to be governed by France.

Much hath been said of the united strength of Britain and the colonies, that in conjunction they might bid defiance to the world. But this is mere presumption; the fate of war is uncertain, neither do the expressions mean any thing; for this continent would never suffer itself to be drained of inhabitants, to support the British arms in either Asia, Africa, or Europe.

Besides, what have we to do with setting the world at defiance? Our plan is commerce, and that, well attended to, will secure us the peace and friendship of all Europe; because, it is the interest of all Europe to have America a *free port.* Her trade will always be a protection, and her barrenness of gold and silver secure her from invaders.

I challenge the warmest advocate for reconciliation, to shew, a single advantage that this continent can reap, by being connected with Great Britain. I repeat the challenge, not a single advantage is derived. Our corn will fetch its price in any market in Europe, and our imported goods must be paid for buy them where we will.

But the injuries and disadvantages we sustain by that connection, are without number; and our duty to mankind at large, as well as to ourselves, instruct us to renounce the alliance: Because, any submission to, or dependance on Great-Britain, tends directly to involve this continent in European wars and quarrels; and sets us at variance with nations, who would otherwise seek our friendship, and against whom, we have neither anger nor complaint. As Europe is our market for trade, we ought to form no partial connection with any part of it. It is the true interest of America to steer clear of European contentions, which she never can do, while by her dependance on Britain, she is made the make-weight in the scale of British politics.

Europe is too thickly planted with kingdoms to be long at peace, and whenever a war breaks out between England and any foreign power, the trade of America goes to ruin, *because of her connection with Britain.* The next war may not turn out like the last, and should it not, the advocates for reconciliation now will be wishing for separation then, because, neutrality in that case, would be a safer convoy than a man of war. Every thing that is right or natural pleads for separation. The blood of the slain, the weeping voice of nature cries, 'Tis TIME TO PART. Even the distance at which the Almighty hath placed England and America, is a strong and natural proof, that the authority of the one, over the other, was never the design of Heaven. The time likewise at which the continent was discovered, adds weight to the argument, and the manner in which it was peopled encreases the force of it. The reformation was preceded by the discovery of America, as if the Almighty graciously meant to open a sanctuary to the persecuted in future years, when home should afford neither friendship nor safety.

The authority of Great-Britain over this continent, is a form of government, which sooner or later must have an end: And a serious mind can draw no true pleasure by looking forward, under the painful and positive conviction, that what he calls "the present constitution" is merely temporary. As parents, we can have no joy, knowing that *this government* is not sufficiently lasting to ensure any thing which we may bequeath to posterity: And by a plain method of argument, as we are running the next generation into debt, we ought to do the work of it, otherwise we use them meanly and pitifully. In order to discover the line of our duty rightly, we should take our children in our hand, and fix our station a few years farther into life; that eminence will present a prospect, which a few present fears and prejudices conceal from our sight.

Though I would carefully avoid giving unnecessary offence, yet I am inclined to believe, that all those who espouse the doctrine of reconciliation, may be included within the following descriptions. Interested men, who are not to be trusted; weak men, who *cannot* see; prejudiced men, who *will not* see; and a certain set of moderate men, who think better of the European world than it deserves; and this last class, by an ill-judged deliberation, will be the cause of more calamities to this continent, than all the other three.

It is the good fortune of many to live distant from the scene of sorrow; the evil is not sufficiently brought to *their* doors to make *them* feel the precariousness with which all American property is possessed. But let our imaginations transport us for a few moments to Boston,[4] that seat of wretchedness will teach us wisdom, and instruct us for ever to renounce a power in whom we can have no trust. The inhabitants of that unfortunate city, who but a few months ago were in ease and affluence, have now, no other alternative than to stay and starve, or turn out to beg. Endangered by the fire of their friends if they continue within the city, and plundered by the soldiery if they leave it. In their present condition they are prisoners without the hope of redemption, and in a general attack for their relief, they would be exposed to the fury of both armies.

Men of passive tempers look somewhat lightly over the offences of Britain, and, still hoping for the best, are apt to call out, *"Come, come, we shall be friends again, for all this."* But examine the passions and feelings of mankind, Bring the doctrine of reconciliation to the touchstone of nature, and then tell me, whether you can hereafter love, honour, and faithfully serve the power that hath carried fire and sword into your land? If you cannot do all these, then are you only deceiving yourselves, and by your delay bringing ruin upon posterity. Your future connection with Britain, whom you can neither love nor honour, will be forced and unnatural, and being formed only on the plan of present convenience, will in a little time fall into a relapse more wretched than the first. But if you say, you can still pass the violations over, then I ask, Hath your house been burnt? Hath your property been destroyed before your face? Are your wife and children destitute of a bed to lie on, or bread to live on? Have you lost a parent or a child by their hands, and yourself the ruined and wretched survivor? If you have not, then are you not a judge of those who have. But if you have, and still can shake hands with the murderers, then are you unworthy the name of husband, father, friend, or lover, and whatever may be

---

[4]British troops had occupied Boston since June 1774. American forces besieged the city from April 19, 1775, until the British evacuated on March 17, 1776.

your rank or title in life, you have the heart of a coward, and the spirit of a sycophant.

This is not inflaming or exaggerating matters, but trying them by those feelings and affections which nature justifies, and without which, we should be incapable of discharging the social duties of life, or enjoying the felicities of it. I mean not to exhibit horror for the purpose of provoking revenge, but to awaken us from fatal and unmanly slumbers, that we may pursue determinately some fixed object. It is not in the power of Britain or of Europe to conquer America, if she do not conquer herself by *delay* and *timidity*. The present winter is worth an age if rightly employed, but if lost or neglected, the whole continent will partake of the misfortune; and there is no punishment which that man will not deserve, be he who, or what, or where he will, that may be the means of sacrificing a season so precious and useful.

It is repugnant to reason, to the universal order of things to all examples from former ages, to suppose, that this continent can longer remain subject to any external power. The most sanguine in Britain does not think so. The utmost stretch of human wisdom cannot, at this time, compass a plan short of separation, which can promise the continent even a year's security. Reconciliation is *now* a falacious dream. Nature hath deserted the connexion, and Art cannot supply her place. For, as Milton wisely expresses, "never can true reconcilement row where wounds of deadly hate have pierced so deep.[5]

Every quiet method for peace hath been ineffectual. Our prayers have been rejected with disdain; and only tended to convince us, that nothing flatters vanity, or confirms obstinacy in Kings more than repeated petitioning—and nothing hath contributed more than that very measure to make the Kings of Europe absolute: Witness Denmark and Sweden. Wherefore, since nothing but blows will do, for God's sake, let us come to a final separation, and not leave the next generation to be cutting throats, under the violated unmeaning names of parent and child.

To say, they will never attempt it again is idle and visionary, we thought so at the repeal of the stamp-act, yet a year or two undeceived us; as well may we suppose that nations, which have been once defeated, will never renew the quarrel.

As to government matters, it is not in the power of Britain to do this continent justice: The business of it will soon be too weighty, and

---

[5] *Paradise Lost* (1667), Book 4.

intricate, to be managed with any tolerable degree of convenience, by a power, so distant from us, and so very ignorant of us; for if they cannot conquer us, they cannot govern us. To be always running three or four thousand miles with a tale or a petition, waiting four or five months for an answer, which when obtained requires five or six more to explain it in, will in a few years be looked upon as folly and childishness—There was a time when it was proper, and there is a proper time for it to cease.

Small islands not capable of protecting themselves, are the proper objects for kingdoms to take under their care; but there is something very absurd, in supposing a continent to be perpetually governed by an island. In no instance hath nature made the satellite larger than its primary planet, and as England and America, with respect to each other, reverses the common order of nature, it is evident they belong to different systems: England to Europe, America to itself.

I am not induced by motives of pride, party, or resentment to espouse the doctrine of separation and independance; I am clearly, positively, and conscientiously persuaded that it is the true interest of this continent to be so; that every thing short of *that* is mere patchwork, that it can afford no lasting felicity,—that it is leaving the sword to our children, and shrinking back at a time, when, a little more, a little farther, would have rendered this continent the glory of the earth.

As Britain hath not manifested the least inclination towards a compromise, we may be assured that no terms can be obtained worthy the acceptance of the continent, or any ways equal to the expence of blood and treasure we have been already put to.

The object, contended for, ought always to bear some just proportion to the expence. The removal of North, or the whole detestable junto, is a matter unworthy the millions we have expended. A temporary stoppage of trade, was an inconvenience, which would have sufficiently ballanced the repeal of all the acts complained of, had such repeals been obtained; but if the whole continent must take up arms, if every man must be a soldier, it is scarcely worth our while to fight against a contemptible ministry only. Dearly, dearly, do we pay for the repeal of the acts, if that is all we fight for; for in a just estimation, it is as great a folly to pay a Bunker-hill price for law, as for land. As I have always considered the independancy of this continent, as an event, which sooner or later must arrive, so from the late rapid progress of the continent to maturity, the event could not be far off. Wherefore, on the breaking out of hostilities, it was not worth the while to have disputed a matter, which time would have finally redressed, unless we meant to be in earnest; otherwise, it is like wasting an estate on a suit at law, to regulate the trespasses of a tenant, whose lease is just expiring. No man was a warmer wisher for reconciliation than myself, before the fatal nineteenth of April 1775,* but the moment the event of that day was made known, I rejected the hardened, sullen tempered Pharoah of England for ever; and disdain the wretch, that with the pretended title of FATHER OF HIS PEOPLE can unfeelingly hear of their slaughter, and composedly sleep with their blood upon his soul.

But admitting that matters were now made up, what would be the event? I answer, the ruin of the continent. And that for several reasons.

First. The powers of governing still remaining in the hands of the king, he will have a negative over the whole legislation of this continent. And as he hath shewn himself such an inveterate enemy to liberty, and discovered such a thirst for arbitrary power; is he, or is he not, a proper man to say to these colonies, *"You shall make no laws but what I please."* And is there any inhabitant in America so ignorant, as not to know, that according to what is called the *present constitution,* that this continent can make no laws but what the king gives leave to; and is there any man so unwise, as not to see, that (considering what has happened) he will suffer no law to be made here, but such as suit *his* purpose. We may be as effectually enslaved by the want of laws in America, as by submitting to laws made for us in England. After matters are made up (as it is called) can there be any doubt, but the whole power of the crown will be exerted, to keep this continent as low and humble as possible? Instead of going forward we shall go backward, or be perpetually quarrelling or ridiculously petitioning.— We are already greater than the king wishes us to be, and will he not hereafter endeavour to make us less? To bring the matter to one point. Is the power who is jealous of our prosperity, a proper power to govern us? Whoever says *No* to this question is an *independant,* for independancy means no more, than, whether we shall make our own laws, or, whether the king, the greatest enemy this continent hath, or can have, shall tell us *"there shall be no laws but such as I like."*

But the king you will say has a negative in England; the people there can make no laws without his consent. In point of right and good order, there is something very ridiculous, that a youth of twenty-one (which hath often happened) shall say to several millions of people, older and wiser than himself, I forbid this or that act of yours to be law. But in this place I decline this sort of reply, though I will never cease to expose the absurdity of it, and only answer, that England

*Massacre at Lexington.

being the King's residence, and America not so, makes quite another case. The king's negative *here* is ten times more dangerous and fatal than it can be in England, for *there* he will scarcely refuse his consent to a bill for putting England into as strong a state of defence as possible, and in America he would never suffer such a bill to be passed.

America is only a secondary object in the system of British politics, England consults the good of *this* country, no farther than it answers her *own* purpose. Wherefore, her own interest leads her to suppress the growth of *ours* in every case which doth not promote her advantage, or in the least interferes with it. A pretty state we should soon be in under such a second-hand government, considering what has happened! Men do not change from enemies to friends by the alteration of a name: And in order to shew that reconciliation *now* is a dangerous doctrine, I affirm, *that it would be policy in the king at this time, to repeal the acts for the sake of reinstating himself in the government of the provinces;* in order, that HE MAY ACCOMPLISH BY CRAFT AND SUBTILTY, IN THE LONG RUN, WHAT HE CANNOT DO BY FORCE AND VIOLENCE IN THE SHORT ONE. Reconciliation and ruin are nearly related.

Secondly. That as even the best terms, which we can expect to obtain, can amount to no more than a temporary expedient, or a kind of government by guardianship, which can last no longer than till the colonies come of age, so the general face and state of things, in the interim, will be unsettled and unpromising. Emigrants of property will not choose to come to a country whose form of government hangs but by a thread, and who is every day tottering on the brink of commotion and disturbance; and numbers of the present inhabitants would lay hold of the interval, to dispose of their effects, and quit the continent.

But the most powerful of all arguments, is, that nothing but independance, i. e. a continental form of government, can keep the peace of the continent and preserve it inviolate from civil wars. I dread the event of a reconciliation with Britain now, as it is more than probable, that it will be followed by a revolt somewhere or other, the consequences of which may be far more fatal than all the malice of Britain.

Thousands are already ruined by British barbarity; (thousands more will probably suffer the same fate) Those men have other feelings than us who have nothing suffered. All they *now* possess is liberty, what they before enjoyed is sacrificed to its service, and having nothing more to lose, they disdain submission. Besides, the general temper of the colonies, towards a British government, will be like that of a youth, who is nearly out of his time; they will care very little about her. And a government which cannot preserve the peace, is no government at all, and in that case we pay our money for nothing; and pray what is it that Britain can do, whose power will be wholly on paper, should a civil tumult break out the very day after reconciliation? I have heard some men say, many of whom I believe spoke without thinking, that they dreaded an independance, fearing that it would produce civil wars. It is but seldom that our first thoughts are truly correct, and that is the case here; for there are ten times more to dread from a patched up connexion than from independance. I make the sufferers case my own, and I protest, that were I driven from house and home, my property destroyed, and my circumstances ruined, that as a man, sensible of injuries, I could never relish the doctrine of reconciliation, or consider myself bound thereby.

The colonies have manifested such a spirit of good order and obedience to continental government, as is sufficient to make every reasonable person easy and happy on that head. No man can assign the least pretence for his fears, on any other grounds, than such as are truly childish and ridiculous, viz. that one colony will be striving for superiority over another.

Where there are no distinctions there can be no superiority, perfect equality affords no temptation. The republics of Europe are all (and we may say always) in peace. Holland and Swisserland are without wars, foreign or domestic: Monarchical governments, it is true, are never long at rest; the crown itself is a temptation to enterprizing ruffians at *home;* and that degree of pride and insolence ever attendant on regal authority, swells into a rupture with foreign powers, in instances, where a republican government, by being formed on more natural principles, would negociate the mistake.

If there is any true cause of fear respecting independance, it is because no plan is yet laid down. Men do not see their way out— Wherefore, as an opening into that business, I offer the following hints; at the same time modestly affirming, that I have no other opinion of them myself, than that they may be the means of giving rise to something better. Could the straggling thoughts of individuals be collected, they would frequently form materials for wise and able men to improve into useful matter.

Let the assemblies be annual, with a President only. The representation more equal. Their business wholly domestic, and subject to the authority of a Continental Congress.

Let each colony be divided into six, eight, or ten, convenient districts, each district to send a proper number of delegates to Congress, so that each colony send at least thirty. The whole number in Congress will be [at] least 390. Each Congress to sit   and to choose a president by the following method. When the delegates are met, let a colony be taken from the whole thirteen colonies by lot, after which, let the whole Congress choose (by ballot) a president from out of the delegates of *that* province. In the next Congress, let a colony be taken by lot from twelve only, omitting that colony from which the president was taken in the former Congress, and so proceeding on till the whole thirteen shall have had their proper rotation. And in order that nothing may pass into a law but what is satisfactorily just, not less than three fifths of the Congress to be called a majority.—He that will promote discord, under a government so equally formed as this, would have joined Lucifer in his revolt.

But as there is a peculiar delicacy, from whom, or in what manner, this business must first arise, and as it seems most agreeable and consistent that it should come from some intermediate body between the governed and the governors, that is, between the Congress and the people, let a CONTINENTAL CONFERENCE be held, in the following manner, and for the following purpose.

A committee of twenty-six members of Congress, viz. two for each colony. Two members from each House of Assembly, or Provincial Convention; and five representatives of the people at large, to be chosen in the capital city or town of each province, for, and in behalf of the whole province, by as many qualified voters as shall think proper to attend from all parts of the province for that purpose; or, if more convenient, the representatives may be chosen in two or three of the most populous parts thereof. In this conference, thus assembled, will be united, the two grand principles of business, *knowledge* and *power.* The members of Congress, Assemblies, or Conventions, by having had experience in national concerns, will be able and useful counsellors, and the whole, being impowered by the people, will have a truly legal authority.

The conferring members being met, let their business be to frame a CONTINENTAL CHARTER, or Charter of the United Colonies; (answering to what is called the Magna Charta of England) fixing the number and manner of choosing members of Congress, members of Assembly, with their date of sitting, and drawing the line of business and jurisdiction between them: (Always remembering, that our strength is continental, not provincial:) Securing freedom and property to all men, and above all things, the free exercise of religion, according to the dictates of conscience; with such other matter as is necessary for a charter to contain. Immediately after which, the said Conference to dissolve, and the bodies which shall be chosen comformable to the said charter, to be the legislators and governors of this continent for the time being: Whose peace and happiness, may God preserve, Amen.

Should any body of men be hereafter delegated for this or some similar purpose, I offer them the following extracts from that wise observer on governments *Dragonetti*. "The science" says he "of the politician consists in fixing the true point of happiness and freedom. Those men would deserve the gratitude of ages, who should discover a mode of government that contained the greatest sum of individual happiness, with the least national expense.

Dragonetti on virtue and rewards."[6]

But where says some is the King of America? I'll tell you Friend, he reigns above, and doth not make havoc of mankind like the Royal Brute of Britain. Yet that we may not appear to be defective even in earthly honors, let a day be solemnly set apart for proclaiming the charter; let it be brought forth placed on the divine law, the word of God; let a crown be placed thereon, by which the world may know, that so far as we approve of monarchy, that in America THE LAW IS KING. For as in absolute governments the King is law, so in free countries the law *ought* to be King; and there ought to be no other. But lest any ill use should afterwards arise, let the crown at the conclusion of the ceremony be demolished, and scattered among the people whose right it is.

A government of our own is our natural right: And when a man seriously reflects on the precariousness of human affairs, he will become convinced, that it is infinitely wiser and safer, to form a constitution of our own in a cool deliberate manner, while we have it in our power, than to trust such an interesting event to time and chance. If we omit it now, some* Massanello may hereafter arise, who laying hold of popular disquietudes, may collect together the desperate and the discontented, and by assuming to themselves the powers of government, may sweep away the liberties of the continent like a deluge. Should the government of America return again into the hands of Britain, the tottering situation of things, will be a temptation for some desperate adventurer to try his fortune; and in such a case, what relief can Britain give? Ere she could hear the news, the fatal business might be done; and ourselves suffering like the wretched Britons under the oppression of the Conqueror. Ye that oppose independance now, ye know not what ye do; ye are opening a door to eternal tyranny, by keeping vacant the seat of government. There

---

[6] Giacinto Dragonetti, *Trattorio delle virtù et de' primi* (1765).

*Thomas Anello, otherwise Massanello, a fisherman from Naples, who after spiriting up his countrymen in the public market place, against the oppression of the Spaniards, to whom the place was then subject, prompted them to revolt, and in the space of a day became king.

are thousands, and tens of thousands, who would think it glorious to expel from the continent, that barbarous and hellish power, which hath stirred up the Indians and Negroes to destroy us, the cruelty hath a double guilt, it is dealing brutally by us, and treacherously by them.

To talk of friendship with those in whom our reason forbids us to have faith, and our affections wounded through a thousand pores instruct us to detest, is madness and folly. Every day wears out the little remains of kindred between us and them, and can there be any reason to hope, that as the relationship expires, the affection will increase, or that we shall agree better, when we have ten times more and greater concerns to quarrel over than ever?

Ye that tell us of harmony and reconciliation, can ye restore to us the time that is past? Can ye give to prostitution its former innocence? Neither can ye reconcile Britain and America. The last cord now is broken, the people of England are presenting addresses against us. There are injuries which nature cannot forgive; she would cease to be nature if she did. As well can the lover forgive the ravisher of his mistress, as the continent forgive the murders of Britain. The Almighty hath implanted in us these unextinguishable feelings for good and wise purposes. They are the guardians of his image in our hearts. They distinguish us from the herd of common animals. The social compact would dissolve, and justice be extirpated from the earth, or have only a casual existence were we callous to the touches of affection. The robber, and the murderer, would often escape unpunished, did not the injuries which our tempers sustain, provoke us into justice.

O ye that love mankind! Ye that dare oppose, not only the tyranny, but the tyrant, stand forth! Every spot of the old world is overrun with oppression. Freedom hath been hunted round the globe. Asia, and Africa, have long expelled her.—Europe regards her like a stranger, and England hath given her warning to depart. O! receive the fugitive, and prepare in time an asylum for mankind.

Of the Present Ability of America, with Some Miscellaneous Reflexions.

I have never met with a man, either in England or America, who hath not confessed his opinion, that a separation between the countries, would take place one time or other: And there is no instance, in which we have shewn less judgment, than in endeavouring to describe, what we call, the ripeness or fitness of the Continent for independance.

As all men allow the measure, and vary only in their opinion of the time, let us, in order to remove mistakes, take a general survey of things, and endeavour, if possible, to find out the *very* time. But we need not go far, the inquiry ceases at once, for, the *time hath found us.* The general concurrence, the glorious union of all things prove the fact.

It is not in numbers, but in unity, that our great strength lies; yet our present numbers are sufficient to repel the force of all the world. The Continent hath, at this time, the largest body of armed and disciplined men of any power under Heaven; and is just arrived at that pitch of strength, in which, no single colony is able to support itself, and the whole, when united, can accomplish the matter, and either more, or, less than this, might be fatal in its effects. Our land force is already sufficient, and as to naval affairs, we cannot be insensible, that Britain would never suffer an American man of war to be built, while the continent remained in her hands. Wherefore, we should be no forwarder an hundred years hence in that branch, than we are now; but the truth is, we should be less so, because the timber of the country is every day diminishing, and that, which will remain at last, will be far off and difficult to procure.

Were the continent crowded with inhabitants, her sufferings under the present circumstances would be intolerable. The more sea port towns we had, the more should we have both to defend and to loose. Our present numbers are so happily proportioned to our wants, that no man need be idle. The diminution of trade affords an army, and the necessities of an army create a new trade.

Debts we have none; and whatever we may contract on this account will serve as a glorious memento of our virtue. Can we but leave posterity with a settled form of government, an independant constitution of its own, the purchase at any price will be cheap. But to expend millions for the sake of getting a few vile acts repealed, and routing the present ministry only, is unworthy the charge, and is using posterity with the utmost cruelty; because it is leaving them the great work to do, and a debt upon their backs, from which, they derive no advantage. Such a thought is unworthy a man of honor, and is the true characteristic of a narrow heart and a pedling politician.

The debt we may contract doth not deserve our regard if the work be but accomplished. No nation ought to be without a debt. A national debt is a national bond; and when it bears no interest, is in no case a grievance. Britain is oppressed with a debt of upwards of one hundred and forty millions sterling, for which she pays upwards of four millions interest. And as a compensation for her debt, she has a large navy; America is without a debt, and without a navy; yet for the twentieth part of the English national debt, could have a navy as large again. The navy of England is not worth, at this time, more than three millions and an half sterling.

The first and second editions of this pamphlet were published without the following calculations, which are now given as a proof that the above estimation of the navy is a just one. *See Entic's naval history, intro.* page 56.[7]

The charge of building a ship of each rate, and furnishing her with masts, yards, sails and rigging, together with a proportion of eight months boatswain's and carpenter's sea-stores, as calculated by Mr. Burchett, Secretary to the navy.

	£.
FOR A SHIP OF A 100 GUNS	35,553
90	29,886
80	23,638
70	17,785
60	14,197
50	10,606
40	7,558
30	5,846
20	3,710

And from hence it is easy to sum up the value, or cost rather, of the whole British navy, which in the year 1757, when it was at its greatest glory consisted of the following ships and guns.

SHIPS.	GUNS.	COST OF ONE.	COST OF ALL.
6	100	35,553 *l.*	213,318 *l.*
12	90	29,886	358,632
12	80	23,638	283,656
43	70	17,785	764,755
35	60	14,197	496,895
40	50	10,606	424,240
45	40	7,558	340,110
58	20	3,710	215,180
85 Sloops, bombs, and fireships, one with another, at		2,000	170,000

Cost 3,266,786

Remains for guns 233,214

3,500,000

[7]John Entick, *A new naval history; or, Compleat view of the British marine* (1757).

No country on the globe is so happily situated, or so internally capable of raising a fleet as America. Tar, timber, iron, and cordage are her natural produce. We need go abroad for nothing. Whereas the Dutch, who make large profits by hiring out their ships of war to the Spaniards and Portuguese, are obliged to import most of the materials they use. We ought to view the building a fleet as an article of commerce, it being the natural manufactory of this country. It is the best money we can lay out. A navy when finished is worth more than it cost. And is that nice point in national policy, in which commerce and protection are united. Let us build; if we want them not, we can sell; and by that means replace our paper currency with ready gold and silver.

In point of manning a fleet, people in general run into great errors; it is not necessary that one fourth part should be sailors. The Terrible privateer, Captain Death, stood the hottest engagement of any ship last war, yet had not twenty sailors on board, though her complement of men was upwards of two hundred. A few able and social sailors will soon instruct a sufficient number of active landmen in the common work of a ship. Wherefore, we never can be more capable to begin on maritime matters than now, while our timber is standing, our fisheries blocked up, and our sailors and shipwrights out of employ. Men of war, of seventy and eighty guns were built forty years ago in New-England, and why not the same now? Ship-building is America's greatest pride, and in which, she will in time excel the whole world. The great empires of the east are mostly inland, and consequently excluded from the possibility of rivalling her. Africa is in a state of barbarism; and no power in Europe, hath either such an extent of coast, or such an internal supply of materials. Where nature hath given the one, she has withheld the other; to America only hath she been liberal of both. The vast empire of Russia is almost shut out from the sea; wherefore, her boundless forests, her tar, iron, and cordage are only articles of commerce.

In point of safety, ought we to be without a fleet? We are not the little people now, which we were sixty years ago; at that time we might have trusted our property in the streets, or fields rather; and slept securely without locks or bolts to our doors or windows. The case now is altered, and our methods of defence, ought to improve with our increase of property. A common pirate, twelve months ago, might have come up the Delaware, and laid the city of Philadelphia under instant contribution, for what sum he pleased; and the same might have happened to other places. Nay, any daring fellow, in a brig of fourteen or sixteen guns, might have robbed the whole Continent, and carried off half a million of money. These are circumstances which demand our attention, and point out the necessity of naval protection.

Some, perhaps, will say, that after we have made it up with Britain, she will protect us. Can we be so unwise as to mean, that she shall keep a navy in our harbours for that purpose? Common sense will tell us, that the power which hath endeavoured to subdue us, is of all others, the most improper to defend us. Conquest may be effected under the pretence of friendship; and ourselves, after a long and brave resistance, be at last cheated into slavery. And if her ships are not to be admitted into our harbours, I would ask, how is she to protect us? A navy three or four thousand miles off can be of little use, and on sudden emergencies, none at all. Wherefore, if we must hereafter protect ourselves, why not do it for ourselves? Why do it for another?

The English list of ships of war, is long and formidable, but not a tenth part of them are at any one time fit for service, numbers of them not in being; yet their names are pompously continued in the list, if only a plank be left of the ship: and not a fifth part, of such as are fit for service, can be spared on any one station at one time. The East, and West Indies, Mediterranean, Africa, and other parts over which Britain extends her claim, make large demands upon her navy. From a mixture of prejudice and inattention, we have contracted a false notion respecting the navy of England, and have talked as if we should have the whole of it to encounter at once, and for that reason, supposed, that we must have one as large; which not being instantly practicable, have been made use of by a set of disguised Tories to discourage our beginning thereon. Nothing can be farther from truth than this; for if America had only a twentieth part of the naval force of Britain, she would be by far an over match for her; because, as we neither have, nor claim any foreign dominion, our whole force would be employed on our own coast, where we should, in the long run, have two to one the advantage of those who had three or four thousand miles to sail over, before they could attack us, and the same distance to return in order to refit and recruit. And although Britain by her fleet, hath a check over our trade to Europe, we have as large a one over her trade to the West Indies, which, by laying in the neighbourhood of the Continent, is entirely at its mercy.

Some method might be fallen on to keep up a naval force in time of peace, if we should not judge it necessary to support a constant navy. If premiums were to be given to merchants, to build and employ in their service, ships mounted with twenty, thirty, forty, or fifty guns, (the premiums to be in proportion to the loss of bulk to the merchants) fifty or sixty of those ships, with a few guard ships on constant duty, would keep up a sufficient navy, and that without burdening ourselves with the evil so loudly complained of in England, of suffering their fleet, in time of peace to lie rotting in the docks. To unite the sinews of commerce and defence is sound policy; for when our strength and our riches, play into each other's hand, we need fear no external enemy.

In almost every article of defence we abound. Hemp flourishes even to rankness, so that we need not want cordage. Our iron is superior to that of other countries. Our small arms equal to any in the world. Cannon we can cast at pleasure. Saltpetre and gunpowder we are every day producing. Our knowledge is hourly improving. Resolution is our inherent character, and courage hath never yet forsaken us. Wherefore, what is it that we want? Why is it that we hesitate? From Britain we can expect nothing but ruin. If she is once admitted to the government of America again, this Continent will not be worth living in. Jealousies will be always arising; insurrections will be constantly happening; and who will go forth to quell them? Who will venture his life to reduce his own countrymen to a foreign obedience? The difference between Pennsylvania and Connecticut, respecting some unlocated lands, shews the insignificance of a British government, and fully proves, that nothing but Continental authority can regulate Continental matters.

Another reason why the present time is preferable to all others, is, that the fewer our numbers are, the more land there is yet unoccupied, which instead of being lavished by the king on his worthless dependants, may be hereafter applied, not only to the discharge of the present debt, but to the constant support of government. No nation under heaven hath such an advantage as this.

The infant state of the Colonies, as it is called, so far from being against, is an argument in favor of independance. We are sufficiently numerous, and were we more so, we might be less united. It is a matter worthy of observation, that the more a country is peopled, the smaller their armies are. In military numbers, the ancients far exceeded the moderns: and the reason is evident, for trade being the consequence of population, men become too much absorbed thereby to attend to any thing else. Commerce diminishes the spirit, both of patriotism, and military defence. And history sufficiently informs us, that the bravest atchievements were always accomplished in the non-age of a nation. With the increase of commerce, England hath lost its spirit. The city of London, notwithstanding its numbers, submits to continued insults with the patience of a coward. The more men have to lose, the less willing are they to venture. The rich are in general slaves to fear, and submit to courtly power with the trembling duplicity of a Spaniel.

Youth is the seed time of good habits, as well in nations as in individuals. It might be difficult, if not impossible, to form the Continent into one government half a century hence. The vast variety of interests, occasioned by an increase of trade and population, would create confusion. Colony would be against colony. Each being able might scorn each other's assistance: and while the proud and foolish gloried in their little distinctions, the wise would lament, that the union had not been formed before. Wherefore, the *present time* is the *true time* for establishing it. The intimacy which is contracted in infancy, and the friendship which is formed in misfortune, are, of all others, the most lasting and unalterable. Our present union is marked with both these characters: we are young, and we have been distressed; but our concord hath withstood our troubles, and fixes a memorable aera for posterity to glory in.

The present time, likewise, is that peculiar time, which never happens to a nation but once, *viz.* the time of forming itself into a government. Most nations have let slip the opportunity, and by that means have been compelled to receive laws from their conquerors, instead of making laws for themselves. First, they had a king, and then a form of government; whereas, the articles or charter of government, should be formed first, and men delegated to execute them afterward: but from the errors of other nations, let us learn wisdom, and lay hold of the present opportunity — *To begin government at the right end.*

When William the Conqueror subdued England, he gave them law at the point of the sword; and until we consent, that the seat of government, in America, be legally and authoritatively occupied, we shall be in danger of having it filled by some fortunate ruffian, who may treat us in the same manner, and then, where will be our freedom? where our property?

As to religion, I hold it to be the indispensible duty of all government, to protect all conscientious professors thereof, and I know of no other business which government hath to do therewith. Let a man throw aside that narrowness of soul, that selfishness of principle, which the niggards of all professions are so unwilling to part with, and he will be at once delivered of his fears on that head. Suspicion is the companion of mean souls, and the bane of all good society. For myself, I fully and conscientiously believe, that it is the will of the Almighty, that there should be diversity of religious opinions among us: It affords a larger field for our Christian kindness. Were we all of one way of thinking, our religious dispositions would want matter for probation; and on this liberal principle, I look on the various denominations among us, to be like children of the same family, differing only, in what is called, their Christian names.

In page thirty-three, I threw out a few thoughts on the propriety of a Continental Charter, (for I only presume to offer hints, not plans) and in this place, I take the liberty of re-mentioning the subject, by observing, that a charter is to be understood as a bond of solemn obligation, which the whole enters into, to support the right of every separate part, whether of religion, personal freedom, or property. A firm bargain and a right reckoning make long friends.

In a former page I likewise mentioned the necessity of a large and equal representation; and there is no political matter which more deserves our attention. A small number of electors, or a small number of representatives, are equally dangerous. But if the number of the representatives be not only small, but unequal, the danger is increased. As an instance of this, I mention the following; when the Associators petition was before the House of Assembly of Pennsylvania; twenty-eight members only were present, all the Bucks county members, being eight, voted against it, and had seven of the Chester members done the same, this whole province had been governed by two counties only, and this danger it is always exposed to. The unwarrantable stretch likewise, which that house made in their last sitting, to gain an undue authority over the Delegates of that province, ought to warn the people at large, how they trust power out of their own hands. A set of instructions for the Delegates were put together, which in point of sense and business would have dishonored a schoolboy, and after being approved by a *few, a very few* without doors, were carried into the House, and there passed *in behalf of the whole colony;* whereas, did the whole colony know, with what ill-will that House hath entered on some necessary public measures, they would not hesitate a moment to think them unworthy of such a trust.

Immediate necessity makes many things convenient, which if continued would grow into oppressions. Expedience and right are different things. When the calamities of America required a consultation, there was no method so ready, or at that time so proper, as to appoint persons from the several Houses of Assembly for that purpose; and the wisdom with which they have proceeded hath preserved this continent from ruin. But as it is more than probable that we shall never be without a CONGRESS, every well wisher to good order, must own, that the mode for choosing members of that body, deserves consideration.

And I put it as a question to those, who make a study of mankind, whether *representation and election* is not too great a power for one and the same body of men to possess? When we are planning for posterity, we ought to remember, that virtue is not hereditary.

It is from our enemies that we often gain excellent maxims, and are frequently surprised into reason by their mistakes. Mr. Cornwall (one of the Lords of the Treasury) treated the petition of the New-York Assembly with contempt, because *that* House, he said, consisted but of twenty-six members, which trifling number, he argued, could not with decency be put for the whole. We thank him for his involuntary honesty.*[8]

To conclude, however strange it may appear to some, or however unwilling they may be to think so, matters not, but many strong and striking reasons may be given, to shew, that nothing can settle our affairs so expeditiously as an open and determined declaration for independance. Some of which are,

First. —It is the custom of nations, when any two are at war, for some other powers, not engaged in the quarrel, to step in as mediators, and bring about the preliminaries of a peace: but while America calls herself the Subject of Great-Britain, no power, however well disposed she may be, can offer her mediation. Wherefore, in our present state we may quarrel on for ever.

Secondly. —It is unreasonable to suppose, that France or Spain will give us any kind of assistance, if we mean only, to make use of that assistance for the purpose of repairing the breach, and strengthening the connection between Britain and America; because, those powers would be sufferers by the consequences.

Thirdly. —While we profess ourselves the subjects of Britain, we must, in the eye of foreign nations, be considered as rebels. The precedent is somewhat dangerous to *their peace,* for men to be in arms under the name of subjects; we, on the spot, can solve the paradox: but to unite resistance and subjection, requires an idea much too refined for common understanding.

Fourthly. —Were a manifesto to be published, and despatched to foreign courts, setting forth the miseries we have endured, and the peaceable methods we have ineffectually used for redress; declaring, at the same time, that not being able, any longer, to live happily or

---

*Those who would fully understand of what great consequence a large and equal representation is to a state, should read Burgh's political Disquisitions.

[8]James Burgh, *Political Disquisitions* (1774).

safely under the cruel disposition of the British court, we had been driven to the necessity of breaking off all connections with her; at the same time, assuring all such courts of our peaceable disposition towards them, and of our desire of entering into trade with them: Such a memorial would produce more good effects to this Continent, than if a ship were freighted with petitions to Britain.

Under our present denomination of British subjects, we can neither be received nor heard abroad: The custom of all courts is against us, and will be so, until, by an independance, we take rank with other nations.

These proceedings may at first appear strange and difficult; but, like all other steps which we have already passed over, will in a little time become familiar and agreeable; and, until an independance is declared, the Continent will feel itself like a man who continues putting off some unpleasant business from day to day, yet knows it must be done, hates to set about it, wishes it over, and is continually haunted with the thoughts of its necessity.

Appendix

Since the publication of the first edition of this pamphlet, or rather, on the same day on which it came out, the King's Speech made its appearance in this city. Had the spirit of prophecy directed the birth of this production, it could not have brought it forth, at a more season-able juncture, or a more necessary time. The bloody mindedness of the one, shew the necessity of pursuing the doctrine of the other. Men read by way of revenge. And the Speech, instead of terrifying, pre-pared a way for the manly principles of Independance.

Ceremony, and even, silence, from whatever motive they may arise, have a hurtful tendency, when they give the least degree of counte-nance to base and wicked performances; wherefore, if this maxim be admitted, it naturally follows, that the King's Speech, as being a piece of finished villany, deserved, and still deserves, a general execration both by the Congress and the people. Yet, as the domestic tranquillity of a nation, depends greatly, on the *chastity* of what may properly be called NATIONAL MANNERS, it is often better, to pass some things over in silent disdain, than to make use of such new methods of dislike, as might introduce the least innovation, on that guardian of our peace and safety. And, perhaps, it is chiefly owing to this prudent delicacy, that the King's Speech, hath not, before now, suffered a public execu-tion. The Speech if it may be called one, is nothing better than a wilful audacious libel against the truth, the common good, and the existence of mankind; and is a formal and pompous method of offering up human sacrifices to the pride of tyrants. But this general massacre of mankind, is one of the privileges, and the certain consequence of Kings; for as nature knows them *not,* they know *not her,* and although they are beings of our *own* creating, they know not *us,* and are become the gods of their creators. The Speech hath one good quality, which is, that it is not calculated to deceive, neither can we, even if we would, be deceived by it. Brutality and tyranny appear on the face of it. It leaves us at no loss: And every line convinces, even in the moment of reading, that He, who hunts the woods for prey, the naked and untutored Indian, is less a Savage than the King of Britain.

Sir John Dalrymple, the putative father of a whining jesuitical piece, fallaciously called, *"The Address of the people of* ENGLAND *to the inhabitants of* AMERICA,*"* hath, perhaps, from a vain supposition, that the people *here* were to be frightened at the pomp and description of a king, given, (though very unwisely on his part) the real character of the present one: "But," says this writer, "if you are inclined to pay compliments to an administration, which we do not complain of," (meaning the Marquis of Rockingham's at the repeal of the Stamp Act) "it is very unfair in you to withhold them from that prince, *by whose* NOD ALONE *they were permitted to do any thing."* This is toryism with a witness! Here is idolatry even without a mask: And he who can calmly hear, and digest such doctrine, hath forfeited his claim to rationality—an apostate from the order of manhood; and ought to be considered—as one, who hath not only given up the proper dignity of man, but sunk himself beneath the rank of animals, and contemptibly crawls through the world like a worm.

However, it matters very little now, what the king of England either says or does; he hath wickedly broken through every moral and human obligation, trampled nature and conscience beneath his feet; and by a steady and constitutional spirit of insolence and cruelty, procure for himself an universal hatred. It is *now* the interest of America to provide for herself. She hath already a large and young family, whom it is more her duty to take care of, than to be granting away her property, to support a power who is become a reproach to the names of men and christians—YE, whose office it is to watch over the morals of a nation, of whatsoever sect or denomination ye are of, as well as ye, who, are more immediately the guardians of the public liberty, if ye wish to preserve your native country uncontaminated by European corruption, ye must in secret wish a separation—But leaving the moral part to private reflection, I shall chiefly confine my farther remarks to the following heads.

First. That it is the interest of America to be separated from Britain.

Secondly. Which is the easiest and most practicable plan, RECONCIL-IATION or INDEPENDANCE? with some occasional remarks.

In support of the first, I could, if I judged it proper, produce the opinion of some of the ablest and most experienced men on this continent; and whose sentiments, on that head, are not yet publicly known. It is in reality a self-evident position: For no nation in a state of foreign dependance, limited in its commerce, and cramped and fettered in its legislative powers, can ever arrive at any material eminence. America doth not yet know what opulence is; and although the progress which she hath made stands unparalleled in the history of other nations, it is but childhood, compared with what she would be capable of arriving at, had she, as she ought to have, the legislative powers in her own hands. England is, at this time, proudly coveting what would do her no good, were she to accomplish it; and the Continent hesitating on a matter, which will be her final ruin if neglected. It is the commerce and not the conquest of America, by which England is to be benefited, and that would in a great measure continue, were the countries as independant of each other as France and Spain; because in many articles, neither can go to a better market. But it is the independance of this country of Britain or any other, which is now the main and only object worthy of contention, and which, like all other truths discovered by necessity, will appear clearer and stronger every day.

First. Because it will come to that one time or other.

Secondly. Because, the longer it is delayed the harder it will be to accomplish.

I have frequently amused myself both in public and private companies, with silently remarking, the specious errors of those who speak without reflecting. And among the many which I have heard, the following seems the most general, viz. that had this rupture happened forty or fifty years hence, instead of *now,* the Continent would have been more able to have shaken off the dependance. To which I reply, that our military ability, *at this time,* arises from the experience gained in the last war, and which in forty or fifty years time, would have been totally extinct. The Continent, would not, by that time, have had a General, or even a military officer left; and we, or those who may succeed us, would have been as ignorant of martial matters as the ancient Indians: And this single position, closely attended to, will unanswerably prove, that the present time is preferable to all others. The argument turns thus—at the conclusion of the last war, we had experience, but wanted numbers; and forty or fifty years hence, we should have numbers, without experience; wherefore, the proper point of time, must be some particular point between the two extremes, in which a sufficiency of the former remains, and a proper increase of the latter is obtained: And that point of time is the present time.

The reader will pardon this digression, as it does not properly come under the head I first set out with, and to which I again return by the following position, viz.

Should affairs be patched up with Britain, and she to remain the governing and sovereign power of America, (which, as matters are now circumstanced, is giving up the point intirely) we shall deprive ourselves of the very means of sinking the debt we have, or may contract. The value of the back lands which some of the provinces are clandestinely deprived of, by the unjust extention of the limits of Canada, valued only at five pounds sterling per hundred acres, amount to upwards of twenty-five millions, Pennsylvania currency; and the quit-rents at one penny sterling per acre, to two millions yearly.

It is by the sale of those lands that the debt may be sunk, without burthen to any, and the quit-rent reserved thereon, will always lessen, and in time, will wholly support the yearly expence of government. It matters not how long the debt is in paying, so that the lands when sold be applied to the discharge of it, and for the execution of which, the Congress for the time being, will be the continental trustees.

I proceed now to the second head, viz. Which is the easiest and most practicable plan, RECONCILIATION or INDEPENDANCE; with some occasional remarks.

He who takes nature for his guide is not easily beaten out of his argument, and on that ground, I answer *generally—That* INDEPENDANCE *being a* SINGLE SIMPLE LINE, *contained within ourselves; and reconciliation, a matter exceedingly perplexed and complicated, and in which, a treacherous capricious court is to interfere, gives the answer without a doubt.*

The present state of America is truly alarming to every man who is capable of reflexion. Without law, without government, without any other mode of power than what is founded on, and granted by courtesy. Held together by an unexampled concurrence of sentiment, which, is nevertheless subject to change, and which, every secret enemy is endeavouring to dissolve. Our present condition, is, Legislation without law; wisdom without a plan; constitution without a name; and, what is strangely astonishing, perfect Independance contending for dependance. The instance is without a precedent; the case never existed before; and who can tell what may be the event? The property of no man is secure in the present unbraced system of things. The mind of the multitude is left at random, and seeing no fixed object before them, they pursue such as fancy or opinion starts. Nothing is criminal; there is no such thing as treason; wherefore, every one thinks himself at liberty to act as he pleases. The Tories dared not have assembled offensively, had they known that their lives, by that act, were forfeited to the laws of the state. A line of distinction should be drawn, between, English soldiers taken in battle, and inhabitants of America taken in arms. The first are prisoners, but the latter traitors. The one forfeits his liberty, the other his head.

Notwithstanding our wisdom, there is a visible feebleness in some of our proceedings which gives encouragement to dissentions. The Continental Belt is too losely buckled. And if something is not done in time, it will be too late to do any thing, and we shall fall into a state, in which, neither *Reconciliation* nor *Independance* will be practicable. The king and his worthless adherents are got at their old game of dividing the Continent, and there are not wanting among us, Printers, who will be busy in spreading specious falsehoods. The artful and hypocritical letter which appeared a few months ago in two of the New-York papers, and likewise in two others, is an evidence that there are men who want either judgment or honesty.

It is easy getting into holes and corners and talking of reconciliation: But do such men seriously consider, how difficult the task is, and how dangerous it may prove, should the Continent divide thereon. Do they take within their view, all the various orders of men whose situation and circumstances, as well as their own, are to be considered therein. Do they put themselves in the place of the sufferer whose *all* is *already* gone, and of the soldier, who hath quitted *all* for the defence of his country. If their ill judged moderation be suited to their own private situations *only,* regardless of others, the event will convince them, that "they are reckoning without their Host."

Put us, say some, on the footing we were on in sixty-three.[9] To which I answer, the request is not *now* in the power of Britain to comply with, neither will she propose it; but if it were, and even should be granted, I ask, as a reasonable question, By what means is such a corrupt and

---

[9]Before the end of the Seven Years War in 1763, Great Britain had not previously, in the memory of American colonists, imposed taxes to raise revenue, as opposed to duties designed to regulate trade.

faithless court to be kept to its engagements? Another parliament, nay, even the present, may hereafter repeal the obligation, on the pretence, of its being violently obtained, or unwisely granted; and in that case, Where is our redress?—No going to law with nations; cannon are the barristers of Crowns; and the sword, not of justice, but of war, decides the suit. To be on the footing of sixty-three, it is not sufficient, that the laws only be put on the same state, but, that our circumstances, likewise, be put on the same state; Our burnt and destroyed towns repaired or built up, our private losses made good, our public debts (contracted for defence) discharged; otherwise, we shall be millions worse than we were at that enviable period. Such a request, had it been complied with a year ago, would have won the heart and soul of the Continent—but now it is too late, "The Rubicon is passed."

Besides, the taking up arms, merely to enforce the repeal of a pecuniary law, seems as unwarrantable by the divine law, and as repugnant to human feelings, as the taking up arms to enforce obedience thereto. The object, on either side, doth not justify the means; for the lives of men are too valuable to be cast away on such trifles. It is the violence which is done and threatened to our persons; the destruction of our property by an armed force; the invasion of our country by fire and sword, which conscientiously qualifies the use of arms: And the instant, in which such a mode of defence became necessary, all subjection to Britain ought to have ceased; and the independancy of America, should have been considered, as dating its aera from, and published by, *the first musket that was fired against her.* This line is a line of consistency; neither drawn by caprice, nor extended by ambition; but produced by a chain of events, of which the colonies were not the authors.

I shall conclude these remarks, with the following timely and well intended hints. We ought to reflect, that there are three different ways, by which an independancy may hereafter be effected; and that *one* of those *three,* will one day or other, be the fate of America, viz. By the legal voice of the people in Congress; by a military power; or by a mob: It may not always happen that our soldiers are citizens, and the multitude a body of reasonable men; virtue, as I have already remarked, is not hereditary, neither is it perpetual. Should an independancy be brought about by the first of those means, we have every opportunity and every encouragement before us, to form the noblest purest constitution on the face of the earth. We have it in our power to begin the world over again. A situation, similar to the present, hath not happened since the days of Noah until now. The birthday of a new world is at hand, and a race of men, perhaps as numerous as all Europe contains, are to receive their portion of freedom from the event of a few months. The Reflexion is awful—and in this point of view, How trifling, how ridiculous, do the little, paltry cavellings, of a few weak or interested men appear, when weighed against the business of a world.

Should we neglect the present favorable and inviting period, and an Independance be hereafter effected by any other means, we must charge the consequence to ourselves, or to those rather, whose narrow and prejudiced souls, are habitually opposing the measure, without either inquiring or reflecting. There are reasons to be given in support of Independance, which men should rather privately think of, than be publicly told of. We ought not now to be debating whether we shall be independant or not, but, anxious to accomplish it on a firm, secure, and honorable basis, and uneasy rather that it is not yet began upon. Every day convinces us of its necessity. Even the Tories (if such beings yet remain among us) should, of all men, be the most solicitous to promote it; for, as the appointment of committees at first, protected them from popular rage, so, a wise and well established form of government, will be the only certain means of continuing it securely to them. *Wherefore,* if they have not virtue enough to be WHIGS, they ought to have prudence enough to wish for Independance.

In short, Independance is the only BOND that can tye and keep us together. We shall then see our object, and our ears will be legally shut against the schemes of an intriguing, as well, as a cruel enemy. We shall then too, be on a proper footing, to treat with Britain; for there is reason to conclude, that the pride of that court, will be less hurt by treating with the American states for terms of peace, than with those, whom she denominates, "rebellious subjects," for terms of accommodation. It is our delaying it that encourages her to hope for conquest, and our backwardness tends only to prolong the war. As we have, without any good effect therefrom, withheld our trade to obtain a redress of our grievances, let us *now* try the alternative, by *independantly* redressing them ourselves, and then offering to open the trade. The mercantile and reasonable part in England, will be still with us; because, peace *with* trade, is preferable to war *without* it. And if this offer be not accepted, other courts may be applied to.

On these grounds I rest the matter. And as no offer hath yet been made to refute the doctrine contained in the former editions of this pamphlet, it is a negative proof, that either the doctrine cannot be refuted, or, that the party in favour of it are too numerous to be opposed. WHEREFORE, instead of gazing at each other with suspicious or doubtful curiosity, let each of us, hold out to his neighbour the hearty hand of friendship, and unite in drawing a line, which, like an act of oblivion shall bury in forgetfulness every former dissention. Let the names of Whig and Tory be extinct; and let none other be heard among us, than those of *a good citizen, an open and resolute friend, and a virtuous supporter of the* RIGHTS *of* MANKIND *and of the* FREE AND INDEPENDANT STATES OF AMERICA.

To the Representatives of the Religious Society of the People called Quakers, or to so many of them as were concerned in publishing a late piece, entitled "The ANCIENT TESTIMONY AND PRINCIPLES of the People called QUAKERS renewed, with Respect to the KING and GOVERNMENT, and touching the COMMOTIONS now prevailing in these and other parts of AMERICA addressed to the PEOPLE IN GENERAL."

THE Writer of this, is one of those few, who never dishonors religion either by ridiculing, or cavilling at any denomination whatsoever. To God, and not to man, are all men accountable on the score of religion. Wherefore, this epistle is not so properly addressed to you as a religious, but as a political body, dabbling in matters, which the professed Quietude of your Principles instruct you not to meddle with.

As you have, without a proper authority for so doing, put yourselves in the place of the whole body of the Quakers, so, the writer of this, in order to be on an equal rank with yourselves, is under the necessity, of putting himself in the place of all those, who, approve the very writings and principles, against which, your testimony is directed: And he hath chosen this singular situation, in order, that you might discover in him that presumption of character which you cannot see in yourselves. For neither he nor you can have any claim or title to *Political Representation.*

When men have departed from the right way, it is no wonder that they stumble and fall. And it is evident from the manner in which ye have managed your testimony, that politics, (as a religious body of men) is not your proper Walk; for however well adapted it might appear to you, it is, nevertheless, a jumble of good and bad put unwisely together, and the conclusion drawn therefrom, both unnatural and unjust.

The two first pages, (and the whole doth not make four) we give you credit for, and expect the same civility from you, because the love and desire of peace is not confined to Quakerism, it is the *natural,* as well the religious wish of all denominations of men. And on this ground, as men laboring to establish an Independant Constitution of our own, do we exceed all others in our hope, end, and aim. *Our plan is peace for ever.* We are tired of contention with Britain, and can see no real end to it but in a final separation. We act consistently, because for the sake of introducing an endless and uninterrupted peace, do we bear the evils and burthens of the present day. We are endeavoring, and will steadily continue to endeavor, to separate and dissolve a connexion which hath already filled our land with blood; and which, while the name of it remains, will be the fatal cause of future mischiefs to both countries.

We fight neither for revenge nor conquest; neither from pride nor passion; we are not insulting the world with our fleets and armies, not ravaging the globe for plunder. Beneath the shade of our own vines are we attacked; in our own houses, and on our own lands, is the violence committed against us. We view our enemies in the character of Highwaymen and Housebreakers, and having no defence for ourselves in the civil law, are obliged to punish them by the military one, and apply the sword, in the very case, where you have before now, applied the halter—Perhaps we feel for the ruined and insulted sufferers in all and every part of the continent, with a degree of tenderness which hath not yet made its way into some of your bosoms. But be ye sure that ye mistake not the cause and ground of your Testimony. Call not coldness of soul, religion; nor put the *Bigot* in the place of the *Christian.*

O ye partial ministers of your own acknowledged principles. If the bearing arms be sinful, the first going to war must be more so, by all the difference between wilful attack and unavoidable defence. Wherefore, if ye really preach from conscience, and mean not to make a political hobby-horse of your religion, convince the world thereof, by proclaiming your doctrine to our enemies, *for they likwise bear* ARMS. Give us proof of your sincerity by publishing it at St. James's, to the commanders in chief at Boston, to the Admirals and Captains who are piratically ravaging our coasts, and to all the murdering miscreants who are acting in authority under HIM whom ye profess to serve. Had ye the honest soul of * *Barclay* ye would preach repentance to *your*

---

*"Thou hast tasted of prosperity and adversity: thou knowest what it is to be banished thy native country, to be over-ruled as well as to rule, and set upon the throne; and being *oppressed* thou hast reason to know how *hateful* the *oppressor* is both to God and man: If after all these warnings and advertisements, thou dost not turn unto the Lord with all thy heart, but forget him who remembered thee in thy distress, and give

king; Ye would tell the Royal Wretch his sins, and warn him of eternal ruin. Ye would not spend your partial invectives against the injured and the insulted only, but, like faithful ministers, would cry aloud and *spare none.* Say not that ye are persecuted, neither endeavour to make us the authors of that reproach, which, ye are bringing upon yourselves; for we testify unto all men, that we do not complain against you because ye are *Quakers,* but because ye pretend to *be* and are NOT Quakers.

Alas! it seems by the particular tendency of some part of your testimony, and other parts of your conduct, as if, all sin was reduced to, and comprehended in, *the act of bearing arms,* and that by the *people only.* Ye appear to us, to have mistaken party for conscience; because, the general tenor of your actions wants uniformity: And it is exceedingly difficult to us to give credit to many of your pretended scruples; because, we see them made by the same men, who, in the very instant that they are exclaiming against the mammon of this world, are nevertheless, hunting after it with a step as steady as Time, and an appetite as keen as Death.

The quotation which ye have made from Proverbs, in the third page of your testimony, that, "when a man's ways please the Lord, he maketh even his enemies to be at peace with him"; is very unwisely chosen on your part; because, it amounts to a proof, that the king's ways (whom ye are so desirous of supporting) do *not* please the Lord, otherwise, his reign would be in peace.

I now proceed to the latter part of your testimony, and that, for which all the foregoing seems only an introduction, viz.

"It hath ever been our judgment and principle, since we were called to profess the light of Christ Jesus, manifested in our consciences unto this day, that the setting up and putting down kings and governments, is God's peculiar prerogative; for causes best known to himself: And that it is not our business to have any hand or contrivance therein; nor to be busy bodies above our station, much less to plot and contrive the ruin, or overturn of any of them, but to pray for the king, and safety of our nation, and good of all men: That we may live a peaceable and quiet life, in all godliness and honesty; *under the government which God is pleased to set over us.*"—If these are *really* your

---

up thyself to follow lust and vanity, surely great will be thy condemnation.—Against which snare, as well as the temptation of those who may or do feed thee, and prompt thee to evil, the most excellent and prevalent remedy will be, to apply thyself to that light of Christ which shineth in thy conscience, and which neither can, nor will flatter thee, nor suffer thee to be at east in thy sins."

Barclay's Address to Charles II.

principles why do ye not abide by them? Why do ye not leave that, which ye call God's Work, to be managed by himself? These very principles instruct you to wait with patience and humility, for the event of all public measures, and to receive *that event* as the divine will towards you. *Wherefore,* what occasion is there for your *political testimony* if you fully believe what it contains: And the very publishing it proves, that either, ye do not believe what ye profess, or have not virtue enough to practise what ye believe.

The principles of Quakerism have a direct tendency to make a man the quiet and inoffensive subject of any, and every government *which is set over him.* And if the setting up and putting down of kings and governments is God's peculiar prerogative, he most certainly will not be robbed thereof by us; wherefore, the principle itself leads you to approve of every thing, which ever happened, or may happen to kings as being his work. OLIVER CROMWELL thanks you. CHARLES, then, died not by the hands of man; and should the present Proud Imitator of him, come to the same untimely end, the writers and publishers of the Testimony, are bound, by the doctrine it contains, to applaud the fact. Kings are not taken away by miracles, neither are changes in governments brought about by any other means than such as are common and human; and such as we are now using. Even the dispersion of the Jews, though foretold by our Saviour, was effected by arms. Wherefore, as ye refuse to be the means on one side, ye ought not to be meddlers on the other; but to wait the issue in silence; and unless ye can produce divine authority, to prove, that the Almighty who hath created and placed this *new* world, at the greatest distance it could possibly stand, east and west, from every part of the old, doth, nevertheless, disapprove of its being independent of the corrupt and abandoned court of Britain, unless I say, ye can shew this, how can ye on the ground of your principles, justify the exciting and stirring up the people "firmly to unite in the *abhorrence* of all such *writings,* and *measures,* as evidence of desire and design to break off the *happy* connexion we have hitherto enjoyed, with the kingdom of Great-Britain, and our just and necessary subordination to the king, and those who are lawfully placed in authority under him." What a slap of the face is here! the men, who in the very paragraph before, have quietly and passively resigned up the ordering, altering, and disposal of kings and governments, into the hands of God, are now, recalling their principles, and putting in for a share of the business. Is it possible, that the conclusion, which is here justly quoted, can any ways follow from the doctrine laid down? The inconsistency is too glaring not to be seen;

the absurdity too great not to be laughed at; and such as could only have been made by those, whose understandings were darkened by the narrow and crabby spirit of a dispairing political party; for ye are not to be considered as the whole body of the Quakers but only as a factional and fractional part thereof.

Here ends the examination of your testimony; (which I call upon no man to abhor, as ye have done, but only to read and judge of fairly;) to which I subjoin the following remark; "That the setting up and putting down of kings," most certainly mean, the making him a king, who is yet not so, and the making him no king who is already one. And pray what hath this to do in the present case? We neither mean to *set up* nor to *put down,* neither to *make* nor to *unmake,* but to have nothing to do with them. Wherefore, your testimony in whatever light it is viewed serves only to dishonor your judgement, and for many other reasons had better have been let alone than published.

First, Because it tends to the decrease and reproach of all religion whatever, and is of the utmost danger to society, to make it a party in political disputes.

Secondly, Because it exhibits a body of men, numbers of whom disavow the publishing political testimonies, as being concerned therein and approvers thereof.

Thirdly, Because it hath a tendency to undo that continental harmony and friendship which yourselves by your late liberal and charitable donations hath lent a hand to establish; and the preservation of which, is of the utmost consequence to us all.

And here without anger or resentment I bid you farewell. Sincerely wishing, that as men and christians, ye may always fully and uninterruptedly enjoy every civil and religious right; and be, in your turn, the means of securing it to others; but that the example which ye have unwisely set, of mingling religion with politics, *may be disavowed and reprobated by every inhabitant of* AMERICA.

7

The Forester, Number 1

April 1, 1776

Despite the controversy over Common Sense, *responses were slow to appear in print. Privately, such conservatives as Thomas Shippen Jr., expressed "shock at the thoughts of it," but the first sustained engagements were those of "Cato," which appeared in eight installments in the* Philadelphia Ledger, *beginning on March 9, 1776. "Cato" was really Dr. William Smith, a leading spokesman for those favoring reconciliation with Great Britain. Smith was, by implication, one of those Paine had characterized in* Common Sense *as among "a certain set of moderate men, who ... will be the cause of more calamities to this continent" (Document 6, p. 91) than all the rest of the Revolution's opponents combined. Cato praised the British constitution, and asked who would protect America from Spain and France if independence was won. He blamed the colonies' troubles on American radicals, like Paine, who usurped rightful authority never delegated to them. Paine's response in the four Forester letters, the first of which is included here, went over much of the same ground he had covered in* Common Sense, *while attacking Cato's style as well as the content of his essays.*

LETTER I

TO CATO

To be *nobly wrong* is more manly than to be *meanly right.* Only let the error be disinterested—let it wear, *not the mask,* but the *mark* of principle and 'tis pardonable. It is on this large and liberal ground, that we distinguish between men and their tenets, and generously preserve our friendship for the one, while we combat with every prejudice of the other. But let not Cato take this compliment to himself; he stands excluded from the benefit of the distinction; he deserves it not—And if the sincerity of disdain can add a cubit to the stature of my sentiments, it shall not be wanting.

Thomas Paine, "Letter I. To Cato," *Pennsylvania Packet,* April 1, 1776.

It is indifferent to me who the writers of Cato's letters are, and sufficient for me to know, that they are gorged with absurdity, confusion, contradiction, and the most notorious and willful falshoods. Let Cato and his faction be against Independance and welcome; their consequence will not *now* turn the scale: But let them have regard to justice, and pay some attention to the plain doctrine of reason. Where these are wanting, the sacred cause of truth applauds our anger, and dignifies it with the name of Virtue.

Four letters have already appeared under the specious name of Cato. What pretensions the writer of them can have to the signature, the Public will best determine; while, on my own part, I prophetically content myself with contemplating the similarity of their exits. The first of those letters promised a second, the second a third, the third a fourth; the fourth hath since made its appearance and still the writer keeps wide of the question. Why doth he thus loiter in the suburbs of the dispute? Why hath he not shewn us what the numerous blessings of reconciliation are, and *proved them practicable?* But he cunningly avoids the point. He cannot but discover the rock he is driving on. The fate of the Roman Cato is before his eyes: And that the Public may be prepared for his funeral, and for his funeral oration, I will venture to predict the time and the manner of his exit. The moment he explains his terms of reconciliation the typographical Cato dies. If they be calculated to please the Cabinet they will not go down with the Colonies; and if they be suited to the Colonies they will be rejected by the Cabinet: The line of no-variation is yet unfound; and, like the philosophers stone, doth not exist. "I am bold," says Cato, "to declare and yet hope to make it evident to every honest man, that the true interest of America lies in *reconciliation* with Great-Britain on *constitutional principles.*"

This is a curious way of lumping the business indeed! And Cato may as well attempt to catch lions in a mouse-trap as to hope to allure the Public with such general and unexplained expressions. It is now a meer bug-bear to talk of *reconciliation* on *constitutional principles,* unless the terms of the first be produced and the sense of the other be defined; and unless he does this he does nothing.

To follow Cato through every absurdity and falshood in the compass of a* letter is impossible; neither is it *now* necessary. *Cassandra* (and I thank him) hath saved me much trouble; there is a spirit in his remarks which honesty only can inspire, and a uniformity in the conduct of his letter which the want of principle can never arrive at. Mark that, Cato.

---

*The writer intended at first to have contained his remarks in one letter.

One observation which I cannot help making on Cato's letters, is, that they are addressed *"To the People of Pennsylvania" only.* In almost any other writer this might have passed unnoticed, but we know it hath mischief in its meaning. The particular circumstance of a Convention is undoubtedly Provincial, but the great business of the day is Continental. And he who dares to endeavour to withdraw this province from the glorious union by which all are supported, deserves the reprobation of all men. It is the true interest of the whole to go hand in hand; and dismal in every instance would be the fate of that Colony which should retreat from the protection of the rest.

The first of Cato's letters is insipid in its stile, language and substance; crouded with personal and private innuendues, and directly levelled against *"the Majesty of the People of Pennsylvania."* The Committee could only call, propose, or recommend a Convention; but, like all other public measures, it still rested with the people at large, whether they would approve it or not; and Cato's reasoning on the right or wrong of that choice is contemptible; because, if the body of the people had thought, or should still think, that the Assembly (or any of their Delegates in Congress) by setting under the embarrassment of *oaths,* and entangled with *Government* and *Governors,* are not so perfectly free as they ought to be, they undoubtedly had, and still have, both the *right* and the *power* to place even the whole authority of the Assembly in any body of men they please; and whoever is hardy enough to say to the contrary is an enemy to mankind. The constitution of Pennsylvania hath been twice changed through the cunning of former Proprietors; surely, the people, whose right, power and property is greater than that of any single man, may make such alterations in their mode of government as the change of times and things require. Cato is exceedingly fond of impressing us with the importance of our *"chartered constitution."* Alas! We are not now, Sir, to be led away by the jingle of a phrase. Had we framed our conduct by the contents of the present charters, we had, ere now, been in a state of helpless misery. That *very assembly* you mention hath broken it, and been obliged to break it, in almost every instance of their proceedings. Hold it up to the Public and it is transparent with holes; pierced with as many deadly wounds as the body of McLeod. Disturb not its remains, Cato, nor dishonour it with another funeral oration.

There is nothing in Cato's first letter worthy of notice but the following insinuating falshood: "Grievous as the least restraint of the press must always be, to a *people* entitled to freedom, it must be the more so, when it is not only unwarranted by *those* to whom they have committed the care of *their* liberties, but cannot be warranted by *them,* consistent with liberty itself."—The rude and unscholastical confusion of persons in the above paragraph, though it throws an obscurity on the meaning, still leaves it discoverable. Who, Sir, hath laid any restraint on the liberty of the press? I know of no instance, in which the press hath been even the object of notice, in this province, except on account of the Tory letter from Kent County which was published last spring in the *Pennsylvania Ledger,* and which it was the duty of every good man to detect, because the *honesty* of the press is as great an object to society as the *freedom* of it. If this is the restraint you complain of we know your true character at once; and that it is so, appears evident from the expression which immediately follows the above quotation; your words are, "Nevertheless, *we* readily submitted to it, while the least colourable pretence could be offered for requiring such a submission." Who submitted, Cato? *we* Whigs or *we* Tories? Until you clear up this, Sir, you must content yourself with being ranked among the rankest of the *writing* Tories; because, no other body of men can have any pretence to complain of want of freedom of the press. It is not your throwing out, now and then, a little popular phrase, which can protect you from suspicion; they are only the gildings under which the poison is conveyed, and without which you dared not to renew your attempts on the virtue of the people.

Cato's second letter, or the greatest part thereof, is taken up with the reverence due from us to the persons and authority of the Commissioners, whom Cato vainly and ridiculously stiles AMBASSADORS *coming to negociate a peace.* How came Cato not to be let a little better into the secret? The act of Parliament which describes the powers of these men, hath been in this city upwards of a month, and in the hands too of Cato's friends. No, Sir, they are not the *Ambassadors of peace,* but the distributors of pardons, mischief and insult. Cato discovers a gross ignorance of the British constitution, in supposing that these men *can* be empowered to act as Ambassadors. To prevent his future errors I will set him right. The present war differs from every other, in this instance, viz. that it is not carried on under the prerogative of the Crown as other wars have always been, but under the authority of the whole legislative power united, and as the barriers which stand in the way of a negociation, are not proclamations but acts of Parliament, it evidently follows, that were even the King of England here in person, he could not ratify the terms or conditions of a reconciliation; because, in the single character of King he could not stipulate for the repeal of *any acts* of Parliament, neither can the Parliament stipulate for him. There is no body of men more jealous of their privileges than the Commons: because they sell them. Mark that, Cato.

I have not the least doubt upon me but that their business (exclusive of granting us pardons) is downright bribery and corruption. It is the machine by which they effect all their plans. We ought to view them as enemies of a most dangerous species, and he who means not to be corrupted by them will enter his protest in time. Are they not the very men who are paid for voting in every measure against us, and ought we not to suspect their designs? Can we view the barbarians as friends? Would it be prudent to trust the viper in our very bosoms? Or to suffer them to ramble at large among us while such doubtful characters as Cato have a being upon the Continent? Yet let their persons be safe from injury and outrage—but trust them not. Our business with them is short and explicit, viz. We are desirous of peace, Gentlemen; we are ready to ratify the terms, and will virtuously fulfil the conditions thereof; but we should deserve all and every misery which tyranny can inflict, were we, after suffering such a repetition of savage barbarities, to come under your government again.

Cato, by way of stealing into credit, says, that "the contest we are engaged in is founded on the most noble and virtuous principles which can animate the mind of man. We are contending, (says he) against an arbitrary Ministry for the rights of Englishmen." No, Cato, we are *now* contending against an arbitrary King to get clear of his tyranny. While the dispute rested in words only, it might be called "contending with the Ministry," but since it is broken out into open war, it is high time to have done with such silly and water-gruel definitions. But it suits not Cato to speak the truth. It is his interest to dress up the sceptered savage in the mildest colours. Cato's patent for a large tract of land is yet unsigned. Alas poor Cato!

Cato proceeds very importantly to tell us, *"that the eyes of all Europe are upon us."* This stale and hackneyed phrase, hath had a regular descent, from many of the King's speeches down to several of the speeches in Parliament; from thence, it took a turn among the little wits and bucks of St. James's; till after suffering all the torture of senseless repetition, and being reduced to a state of vagrancy, was charitably picked up to embellish the second letter of Cato. It is truly of the bug-bear kind, contains no meaning, and the very using it discovers a barrenness of invention. It signifies nothing to tell us "that the eyes of all Europe are upon us," unless he had likewise told us what they are looking at us *for;* which, as he hath not done, I will:

They are looking at us, Cato, in hopes of seeing a final separation between Britain and the Colonies, that they, the *lookers on,* may partake of a free and uninterrupted trade with the whole Continent of America. Cato! thou reasonest *wrong.*

For the present, Sir, farewell. I have seen thy soliloquy and despise it. Remember, thou hast thrown me the glove, Cato, and either thee or I must tire. I fear not the field of fair debate, but thou hast stepped aside and made it personal—Thou hast tauntingly called on me by name; and if I cease to hunt thee from every lane and lurking-hole of mischief, and bring thee not a trembling culprit before the public bar, then brand me with reproach, by naming me in the list of your confederates.

Philadelphia, March 28, 1776.   THE FORESTER.

8

The American Crisis, Number 1
December 19, 1776

A higher percentage of enlisted men died in the American Revolution than in any other war except the Civil War. The Revolution was even more of a civil war than the one that bears the name, as neighbor fought against neighbor, relative against relative, and all regions—North and South, East and West—saw heavy fighting. There was bloodshed before 1776, most famously at Lexington and Concord, in Massachusetts, but 1776 was the first full year of what would be a very long and brutal war. The Patriot side did not fare well in that first year and there was a very real possibility that the British would win early and decisively. The first setback for the Patriot cause came in Canada, where the American siege of Quebec failed. The core of the continental army under General George Washington was about 19,000 men, which moved from Boston to New York to face more than 30,000 British troops under General William Howe. The Americans were routed from Long Island, chased to Brooklyn Heights, and evacuated to Manhattan during September. In October, Washington's army was driven out of Manhattan and Westchester. In

Thomas Paine, *The American Crisis, Number 1* (Philadelphia: Styner and Cist Printing, 1776).

November, the Americans fled from Fort Lee, on the New Jersey side of the Hudson River, and continued south with the British in hot pursuit, eventually crossing the Delaware River to Pennsylvania, where the British were content to leave what was left of Washington's tattered army for the winter. Cold, exhausted, and demoralized, with enlistments due to expire at the end of the year, only 6,000 of what had been a 27,000-man army remained. Even Thomas Jefferson speculated about acceptable terms of surrender. It was at this critical moment that the first of Thomas Paine's American Crisis *letters appeared. And it was to this army that Paine addressed his powerful words.*

These are the times that try men's souls: The summer soldier and the sunshine patriot will, in this crisis, shrink from the service of his country; but he that stands it NOW, deserves the love and thanks of man and woman. Tyranny, like hell, is not easily conquered; yet we have this consolation with us, that the harder the conflict, the more glorious the triumph. What we obtain too cheap, we esteem too lightly:—'Tis dearness only that gives every thing its value. Heaven knows how to set a proper price upon its goods; and it would be strange indeed, if so celestial an article as FREEDOM should not be highly rated. Britain, with an army to enforce her tyranny, has declared, that she has a right (*not only to* TAX) but *"to* BIND *us in* ALL CASES WHATSOEVER," and if being *bound in that manner is* not slavery, then is there not such a thing as slavery upon earth. Even the expression is impious, for so unlimited a power can belong only to GOD.

Whether the Independence of the Continent was declared too soon, or delayed too long, I will not now enter into as an argument; my own simple opinion is, that had it been eight months earlier, it would have been much better. We did not make a proper use of last winter, neither could we, while we were in a dependent state. However, the fault, if it were one, was all our own; we have none to blame but ourselves.* But no great deal is lost yet; all that Howe has been doing for this month past is rather a ravage than a conquest, which the spirit of the Jersies

---

*"The present winter" (meaning the last) "is worth an age, if rightly employed, but if lost, or neglected, the whole Continent will partake of the evil; and there is no punishment that man does not deserve, be he who, or what, or where he will, that may be the means of sacrificing a season so precious and useful." COMMON SENSE.

a year ago would have quickly repulsed, and which time and a little resolution will soon recover.

I have as little superstition in me as any man living, but my secret opinion has ever been, and still is, that GOD almighty will not give up a people to military destruction, or leave them unsupportedly to perish, who had so earnestly and so repeatedly sought to avoid the calamities of war, by every decent method which wisdom could invent. Neither have I so much of the infidel in me, as to suppose, that HE has relinquished the government of the world, and given us up to the care of devils; and as I do not, I cannot see on what grounds the king of Britain can look up to heaven for help against us: A common murderer, a highwayman, or a housebreaker, has as good a pretence as he.

'Tis surprising to see how rapidly a panic will sometimes run through a country. All nations and ages have been subject to them: Britain has trembled like an ague at the report of a French fleet of flat bottomed boats; and in the fourteenth century the whole English army, after ravaging the kingdom of France, was driven back like men petrified with fear; and this brave exploit was performed by a few broken forces collected and headed by a woman, Joan of Arc. Would, that Heaven might inspire some Jersey maid to spirit up her countrymen, and save her fair fellow-sufferers from ravage and ravishment! Yet panics, in some cases, have their uses; they produce as much good as hurt. Their duration is always short; the mind soon grows thro' them, and acquires a firmer habit than before. But their peculiar advantage is, that they are the touchstones of sincerity and hypocrisy, and bring things and men to light, which might otherwise have lain for ever undiscovered. In fact, they have the same effect on secret traitors, which an imaginary apparition would upon a private murderer. They sift out the hidden thoughts of man, and hold them up in public to the world. Many a disguised Tory has lately shewn his head, that shall penitentially solemnize with curses the day on which Howe arrived upon the Delaware.

As I was with the troops at Fort Lee, and marched with them to the edge of Pennsylvania, I am well acquainted with many circumstances, which those, who lived at a distance, know but little or nothing of. Our situation there was exceedingly cramped, the place being on a narrow neck of land between the North river and the Hackensack. Our force was inconsiderable, being not one fourth so great as Howe could bring against us. We had no army at hand to have relieved the garrison, had we shut ourselves up and stood on the defence. Our ammunition, light artillery, and the best part of our stores, had been removed upon the apprehension that Howe would endeavor to penetrate the Jersies, in which case Fort Lee could be of no use to us; for it must occur to every thinking man, whether in the army or not, that these kind of field forts are only for temporary purposes, and last in use no longer than the enemy directs his force against the particular object, which such forts are raised to defend. Such was our situation and condition at Fort Lee on the morning of the 20th of November, when an officer arrived with information, that the enemy with 200 boats had landed about seven or eight miles above: Major General Green, who commanded the garrison, immediately ordered them under arms, and sent express to his Excellency General Washington at the town of Hackensack, distant by the way of the ferry six miles. Our first object was to secure the bridge over the Hackensack, which laid up the river between the enemy and us, about six miles from us and three from them. General Washington arrived in about three quarters of an hour, and marched at the head of the troops towards the bridge, which place I expected we should have a brush for; however they did not chuse to dispute it with us, and the greatest part of our troops went over the bridge, the rest over the ferry, except some which passed at a mill on a small creek, between the bridge and the ferry, and made their way through some marshy grounds up to the town of Hackensack, and there passed the river. We brought off as much baggage as the waggons could contain, the rest was lost. The simple object was to bring off the garrison, and to march them on till they could be strengthened by the Jersey or Pennsylvania militia, so as to be enabled to make a stand. We staid four days at Newark, collected in our outposts with some of the Jersey militia, and marched out twice to meet the enemy on information of their being advancing, though our numbers were greatly inferiour to theirs. Howe, in my little opinion, committed a great error in generalship, in not throwing a body of forces off from Staaten Island through Amboy, by which means he might have seized all our stores at Brunswick, and intercepted our march into Pennsylvania: But, if we believe the power of hell to be limited, we must likewise believe that their agents are under some providential controul.

I shall not now attempt to give all the particulars of our retreat to the Delaware; suffice it for the present to say, that both officers and men, though greatly harassed and fatigued, frequently without rest, covering, or provision, the inevitable consequences of a long retreat, bore it with a manly and a martial spirit. All their wishes were one, which was, that the country would turn out and help them to drive the enemy back. Voltaire has remarked, that king William never appeared to full advantage but in difficulties and in action; the same remark may be made on General Washington, for the character fits him. There is a natural firmness in some minds which cannot be unlocked by triffles, but which, when unlocked, discovers a cabinet of fortitude; and I reckon it among those kind of public blessings, which we do not immediately see, that GOD hath blest him with uninterrupted health, and given him a mind that can even flourish upon care.

I shall conclude this paper with some miscellaneous remarks on the state of our affairs; and shall begin with asking the following question, Why is it that the enemy hath left the New-England provinces, and made these middle ones the seat of war? The answer is easy: New-England is not infested with Tories, and we are. I have been tender in raising the cry against these men, and used numberless arguments to shew them their danger, but it will not do to sacrifice a world to either their folly or their baseness. The period is now arrived, in which either they or we must change our sentiments, or one or both must fall. And what is a Tory? Good GOD! what is he? I should not be afraid to go with a hundred Whigs against a thousand Tories, were they to attempt to get into arms. Every Tory is a coward, for a servile, slavish, self-interested fear is the foundation of Toryism; and a man under such influence, though he may be cruel, never can be brave.

But before the line of irrecoverable separation be drawn between us, let us reason the matter together: Your conduct is an invitation to the enemy, yet not one in a thousand of you has heart enough to join him. Howe is as much deceived by you as the American cause is injured by you. He expects you will all take up arms, and flock to his standard with muskets on your shoulders. Your opinions are of no use to him, unless you support him personally; for 'tis soldiers, and not Tories, that he wants.

I once felt all that kind of anger, which a man ought to feel, against the mean principles that are held by the Tories: A noted one, who kept a tavern at Amboy, was standing at his door, with as pretty a child in his hand, about eight or nine years old, as most I ever saw, and after speaking his mind as freely as he thought was prudent, finished with this unfatherly expression, *"Well! give me peace in my day."* Not a man lives on the Continent but fully believes that a seperation must some time or other finally take place, and a generous parent would have said, *"If there must be trouble, let it be in my day, that my child may have peace;"* and this single reflection, well applied, is sufficient to awaken every man to duty. Not a place upon earth might be so happy as America. Her situation is remote from all the wrangling world, and she has nothing to do but to trade with them. A man may easily distinguish in himself between temper and principle, and I am as confident, as I am that GOD governs the world, that America will never be happy till she gets clear of foreign dominion. Wars, without ceasing, will break out till that period arrives, and the Continent must in the end be conqueror; for, though the flame of liberty may sometimes cease to shine, the coal never can expire.

America did not, nor does not, want force; but she wanted a proper application of that force. Wisdom is not the purchase of a day, and it is no wonder that we should err at first sitting off. From an excess of tenderness, we were unwilling to raise an army, and trusted our cause to the temporary defence of a well meaning militia. A summer's experience has now taught us better; yet with those troops, while they were collected, we were able to set bounds to the progress of the enemy, and, thank GOD! they are again assembling. I always considered a militia as the best troops in the world for a sudden exertion, but they will not do for a long campaign. Howe, it is probable, will make an attempt on this city; should he fail on this side the Delaware, he is ruined; if he succeeds, our cause is not ruined. He stakes all on his side against a part of ours; admitting he succeeds, the consequence will be, that armies from both ends of the Continent will march to assist their suffering friends in the middle States; for he cannot go every where, it is impossible. I consider Howe as the greatest enemy the Tories have; he is bringing a war into their country, which, had it not been for him and partly for themselves, they had been clear of. Should he now be expelled, I wish, with all the devotion of a Christian, that the names of Whig and Tory may never more be mentioned; but should the Tories give him encouragement to come, or assistance if he come, I as sincerely wish that our next year's arms may expell them from the Continent, and the Congress appropriate their possessions to the relief of those who have suffered in well doing. A single successful battle next year will settle the whole. America could carry on a two years war by the confiscation of the property of disaffected persons, and be made happy by their expulsion. Say not that this is revenge, call it rather the soft resentment of a suffering people, who, having no object in view but the GOOD of ALL, have staked their OWN ALL upon a seemingly doubtful event. Yet it is folly to argue against determined hardness; eloquence may strike the ear, and the language of sorrow draw forth the tear of compassion, but nothing can reach the heart that is steeled with prejudice.

Quitting this class of men, I turn with the warm ardour of a friend to those who have nobly stood, and are yet determined to stand the matter out: I call not upon a few, but upon all; not on THIS State or THAT State, but on EVERY State; up and help us; lay your shoulders to the wheel; better have too much force than too little, when so great an object is at stake. Let it be told to the future world, that in the depth of winter, when nothing but hope and virtue could survive, that the city and the country, alarmed at one common danger, came forth to meet and to repulse it. Say not, that thousands are gone, turn out your tens of thousands; throw not the burthen of the day upon Providence, but *"shew your faith by your works,"* that GOD may bless you. It matters not where you live, or what rank of life you hold, the evil or the blessing will reach you all. The far and the near, the home counties and the back, the rich and the poor, shall suffer or rejoice alike. The heart that feels not now, is dead: The blood of his children shall curse his cowardice, who shrinks back at a time when a little might have saved the whole, and made *them* happy. I love the man that can smile in trouble, that can gather strength from distress, and grow brave by reflection. 'Tis the business of little minds to shrink; but he whose heart is firm, and whose conscience approves his conduct, will pursue his principles unto death. My own line of reasoning is to myself as strait and clear as a ray of light. Not all the treasures of the world, so far as I believe, could have induced me to support an offensive war, for I think it murder; but if a thief break into my house, burn and destroy my property, and kill or threaten to kill me, or those that are in it, and to *"bind me in all cases whatsoever,"* to his absolute will, am I to suffer it? What signifies it to me, whether he who does it, is a king or a common man; my countryman or not my countryman? whether it is done by an individual villain, or an army of them? If we reason to the root of things we shall find no difference; neither can any just cause be assigned why we should punish in the one case, and pardon in the other. Let them call me rebel, and welcome, I feel no concern from it; but I should suffer the misery of devils, were I to make a whore of my soul by swearing allegiance to one, whose character is that of a sottish, stupid, stubborn, worthless, brutish man. I conceive likewise a horrid idea in receiving mercy from a being, who at the last day shall be shrieking to the rocks and mountains to cover him, and fleeing with terror from the orphan, the widow and the slain of America.

There are cases which cannot be overdone by language, and this is one. There are persons too who see not the full extent of the evil that threatens them; they solace themselves with hopes that the enemy, if they succeed, will be merciful. It is the madness of folly to expect mercy from those who have refused to do justice; and even mercy, where conquest is the object, is only a trick of war: The cunning of the fox is as murderous as the violence of the wolfe; and we ought to guard equally against both. Howe's first object is partly by threats and partly by promises, to terrify or seduce the people to deliver up their arms, and receive mercy. The ministry recommended the same plan to Gage, and this is what the Tories call making their peace; *"a peace which passeth all understanding" indeed!* A peace which would be the immediate forerunner of a worse ruin than any we have yet thought of. Ye men of Pennsylvania, do reason upon those things! Were the back counties to give up their arms, they would fall an easy prey to the Indians, who are all armed: This perhaps is what some Tories would not be sorry for. Were the home counties to deliver up their arms, they would be exposed to the resentment of the back counties, who would then have it in their power to chastise their defection at pleasure. And were any one State to give up its arms, THAT State must be garrisoned by all Howe's army of Britons and Hessians to preserve it from the anger of the rest. Mutual fear is a principal link in the chain of mutual love, and woe be to that State that breaks the compact. Howe is mercifully inviting you to barbarous destruction, and men must be either rogues or fools that will not see it. I dwell not upon the vapours of imagination; I bring reason to your ears; and in language, as plain as A, B, C, hold up truth to your eyes.

I thank GOD that I fear not. I see no real cause for fear. I know our situation well, and can see the way out of it. While our army was collected, Howe dared not risk a battle, and it is no credit to him that he decamped from the White Plains, and waited a mean opportunity to ravage the defenceless Jersies; but it is great credit to us, that, with an handful of men, we sustained an orderly retreat for near an hundred miles, brought off our ammunition, all our field-pieces, the greatest part of our stores, and had four rivers to pass. None can say that our retreat was precipitate, for we were near three weeks in performing it, that the country might have time to come in. Twice we marched back to meet the enemy and remained out till dark. The sign of fear was not seen in our camp, and had not some of the cowardly and disaffected inhabitants spread false alarms thro' the country, the Jersies had never been ravaged. Once more we are again collected and collecting; our new army at both ends of the Continent is recruiting fast, and we shall be able to open the next campaign with sixty thousand men, well armed and cloathed. This is our situation, and who will may know it. By perseverance and fortitude we have the prospect of a glorious issue; by cowardice and submission, the sad choice of a variety of evils—a ravaged country—a depopulated city—habitations without safety, and slavery without hope—our homes turned into barracks and baudy-houses for Hessians, and a future race to provide for whose fathers we shall doubt of. Look on this picture, and weep over it—and if there yet remains one thoughtless wretch who believes it not, let him suffer it unlamented.

A Thomas Paine Chronology
(1737–1819)

1737 Born January 29 in Thetford, Norfolk, England, to Frances Cocke Pain (b. 1697), Anglican daughter of an attorney, and Joseph Pain (1708–1786), a Quaker corset maker.

1738 Sister Elizabeth born August 29 and dies in infancy.

1743 Begins attending Thetford grammar school.

1750 Leaves school to begin apprenticeship in father's shop.

1757 Serves on privateer *King of Prussia* for six months.

1758 Moves to Dover, Kent, where he works as a corset maker.

1759 Opens corset-making shop in Sandwich and marries Mary Lambert, an orphan working as a maid, on September 27.

1760 Wife dies in childbirth.

1762– 1763 Begins work as an excise tax collector assigned to Grantham, Lincolnshire.

1765 Dismissed from excise position in August, returns to corset making in Diss, Norfolk.

1766 Moves to London and teaches in a private academy.

1767 Teaches at a school in Kensington.

1768 Is reappointed an excise officer after appeal and begins work in Lewes, Sussex.

1769– 1770 Begins running tobacco shop of deceased former landlord, Samuel Ollive, while continuing as excise officer.

1771 Marries Elizabeth Ollive (b. 1749), daughter of Samuel Ollive and his widow, on March 26.

1772– 1773 Joins petitioning movement for higher wages for excise officers. Writes pamphlet *The Case of the Officers of Excise* and spends winter in London distributing pamphlet to members of parliament. Parliament takes no action in response to petitioning officers.

1774 Dismissed from excise service on April 8 for being absent from his assigned position in Lewes without permission. Tobacco shop fails. Signs formal separation with wife on June 4. Travels to London, where he is introduced to Benjamin Franklin. Sails for Philadelphia in early October. Arrives in Philadelphia in early December.

1775 Secures job writing and editing *The Pennsylvania Magazine: Or American Monthly Museum,* published by Robert Aitken. Leaves job in September, discontented with financial arrangements. Writes *Common Sense* during fall.

1776 *Common Sense* published January 10; expanded edition February 14. Writes "Forester" letters published in Pennsylvania newspapers. Joins Pennsylvania militia and serves in "Flying Camp" under General Daniel Roberdeau. In September, becomes aide-de-camp to General Nathaniel Greene at Fort Lee, New Jersey. Writes reports on war for Philadelphia newspapers and begins work on first of thirteen essays called *The American Crisis,* which is published in Philadelphia on December 19.

1777 Publishes *The American Crisis* numbers 2, 3, and 4. Appointed Pennsylvania's observer with General Washington's army in October.

1778 Writes *The American Crisis* numbers 6 and 7. Also writes in support of Pennsylvania Constitution of 1776. Writes a series of essays attacking Silas Deane, a Connecticut merchant who was sent to France to purchase supplies, accusing Deane of profiteering.

1779 Writes ever more hostile attacks on Deane. Eventually resigns as secretary of the Continental Congress's committee for foreign affairs, having embarrassed Congress in its relations with France by revelations of corrupt dealings.

1780 Publishes *The American Crisis* numbers 8 and 9, and *The Crisis Extraordinary.* Writes and publishes *The Public Good,* which contested Virginia's claim to western territories and urged their session to Congress.

1781 Accompanies John Laurens to France on a mission to gain further loans and supplies in support of the American war.

1782 Writes *The American Crisis* number 11. Enters into secret contract to write in support of financial measures pursued by financier Robert Morris.

1783 Writes and publishes *The Last Crisis,* misnumbered 13, on April 19, the eighth anniversary of the battle of Lexington and Concord.

1785 Elected to membership in American Philosophical Society. Works on inventions of smokeless candles and single-span iron bridge.

1787   Exhibits model of his wrought-iron bridge in Philadelphia. Sails for France on April 26; lands on May 26 and goes to Paris. Presents bridge model to the French Academy of Sciences. Meets and begins friendship with Thomas Jefferson. Travels to London, seeking endorsement of his bridge by the Royal Society. Sees his mother in Thetford and establishes an annuity for her, his father having died the previous year. Returns to Paris in December.

1788   Returns to England and supervises construction of a ninety-foot bridge arch.

1789   Continues work on bridge. In August the National Assembly of France adopts the Declaration of the Rights of Man and Citizen. Paine returns to Paris.

1790   Edmund Burke, leading English literary figure and politician, publishes *Reflections on the Revolution in France,* which sells 12,000 copies in a month.

1791   Paine's *Rights of Man: Being an Answer to Mr. Burke's Attack on the French Revolution* published in London on February 22 and then withdrawn, apparently due to publisher's fear of prosecution for treason. Pamphlet reissued by another publisher and sells tens of thousands of copies. A hostile biography, *Life of Thomas Pain,* by George Chalmers writing under the pseudonym of Francis Oldys is published in London.

1792   Paine publishes *Rights of Man, Part the Second, Combining Principle and Practice* in London. Sales of first and second parts exceed 200,000 copies by end of year. London crowds hang and burn effigies of Paine. On December 18, Paine is convicted in absentia of seditious libel in a London trial. English government begins prosecuting printers and sellers of *Rights of Man.*

1793   Louis XVI beheaded on January 21. Paine tries to stay out of French politics and drinks heavily. Works during fall on *Age of Reason,* his deistic views on religion. Arrested in Paris on December 28, as the French Revolution takes turn that he does not fully comprehend.

1794   In January *The Age of Reason: Being an Investigation of True and of Fabulous Theology* is published in Paris. Appeals for Paine's release from prison on grounds that he is an American citizen are rejected because he had accepted French citizenship and had a seat in the Convention. Released from prison on November 4 in response to American Ambassador James Monroe's appeal.

1795   Writes angry letter to President George Washington for not getting him released from prison. Publishes *Dissertation on First Principles of Government,* which supports universal manhood suffrage.

In August, finishes second part of *Age of Reason,* which contains an attack on the authority of the Bible. Writes *Agrarian Justice,* which supports taxing land and compensating those who do not inherit land.

1796 Publishes *The Decline and Fall of the English System of Finance,* which predicts the failure of the Bank of England. Writes enraged public letter to George Washington, which accuses the outgoing president of treachery, hypocrisy, and being a bad general in the Revolution.

1797 *Agrarian Justice, Opposed to Agrarian Law, and to Agrarian Monopoly* published.

1801 Thomas Jefferson inaugurated as third president of the United States and writes to Paine in March offering him passage on an American warship.

1802 Sails from Le Havre in September and lands in Baltimore on October 30. Attacked in the American press as a drunkard and an atheist. Jefferson receives him at the White House nonetheless. Publishes a series of letters "To the Citizens of the United States" in which he attacks George Washington (who died several years earlier) and John Adams.

1802–
1803 Old friends Samuel Adams and Benjamin Rush estranged from him because of the religious views published in *The Age of Reason.* Hostile reception by crowd in Trenton, New Jersey. Received more favorably at a dinner in his honor in New York. Resides in New Rochelle, New York, where he owns a small farm. Falls ill.

1804–
1805 Drinks heavily as health deteriorates.

1806 His citizenship questioned by New Rochelle election officials, who refuse to count his ballot. Moves to Manhattan.

1808 Begins boarding in a house in Greenwich Village. Loses use of his legs.

1809 Makes out will in January. Requires constant medical care. Develops severe swelling and painful skin sores. Society of Friends denies his request to be buried in a Quaker cemetery. Refuses pleas that he recant deism and accept Christianity before his death. Dies June 8. Buried on New Rochelle farm.

1819 English journalist William Cobbett has Paine's bones exhumed and returned to England, intending to build a memorial to him. The plan fails and the bones are eventually lost.

Questions for Consideration

AFRICAN SLAVERY IN AMERICA

1. What are the justifications for slavery that Paine argued against in this essay?

2. What were Paine's sources—Biblical, legal, historical, moral, and logical—for his argument in favor of the immediate abolition of slavery?

3. What practical problems would the Pennsylvanians face if they followed Paine's advice to free their slaves? How did Paine believe these problems could be resolved?

4. How do you imagine that this essay made its readers feel?

A SERIOUS THOUGHT

1. How did Paine characterize the British colonization of the Americas?

2. What makes Americans more moral than the British in Paine's telling of the history of colonization?

3. As Paine explained it, what moral responsibilities would fall on the Americans once they were free of Great Britain?

4. According to Paine, would this moral responsibility extend to the Indians and Africans who lived in the United States or only to the slaves not yet imported?

A DIALOGUE BETWEEN GENERAL WOLFE
AND GENERAL GAGE IN A WOOD NEAR BOSTON

1. To whom, according to Paine, is a military leader responsible?

2. In a case where a military leader's responsibilities to different constituencies conflict, what is his highest or first responsibility?

3. How does Paine explain this highest responsiblity? What are the grounds of Wolfe's position?

THOUGHTS ON DEFENSIVE WAR

1. What was Paine's definition of *defensive war?*
2. What is the meaning of *liberty* as Paine used the term?
3. Why must Americans fight the British *now?*

REFLECTIONS ON UNHAPPY MARRIAGES

1. What, according to Paine, was the best way to choose a marriage partner?
2. Regarding this choice, does Paine believe women and men have different roles and responsibilities?
3. What did Paine believe made a happy marriage?
4. Why, according to Paine, do Indians have happier marriages than Europeans?
5. What roles do freedom and equality, principles that Paine applied to social and political contexts, play in marriages?

COMMON SENSE

1. Why is "nature" on the Americans' side in the revolution that Paine advocated in *Common Sense*?
2. How, according to Paine, does nature disprove the hereditary right of kings?
3. What was wrong, in Paine's opinion, with the "so much boasted constitution of England"? How do his ideas about the British constitution compare with his ideas about nature?
4. How did Paine's belief that even the best government is evil affect his proposed design for a new government?
5. When Paine wrote that "I draw my idea of the form of government from a principle of nature," what is the principle? What does this natural government look like, and how is it different from the one that Americans had at that time?
6. According to Paine, to what did America owe its past, present, and future economic prosperity?
7. How would the revolution that Paine proposed make American society more moral?
8. What, in Paine's opinion, was the problem with monarchy?
9. Why did Paine state that the model of balanced government is "farcical" in both design and execution?

10. If the general purpose of government is "rendered necessary by the inability of moral virtue to govern the world," what specific ends of governments must any design take into account, according to Paine?

11. What do you think Paine meant by "Time makes more converts than reason"? What is the significance of that observation?

12. To what audience is *Common Sense* addressed?

13. What did Paine mean by "equality"?

14. Why did Paine believe that Americans had a duty to humanity to break free from Great Britain?

15. Why did Paine think that a national debt is good for a country?

THE FORESTER, NUMBER 1

1. To what specific criticisms of *Common Sense* did Paine respond in this letter?

2. What vocabulary did this letter share with *Common Sense*?

3. What stylistic similarities can you find between this letter and Paine's other writings from 1775 and 1776?

4. How did Paine link Cato's writing style and the substance of what Cato had to say?

5. Is it possible that Cato was not a Loyalist, but a supporter of the Revolutionary movement?

THE AMERICAN CRISIS, NUMBER 1

1. What similarities and differences do you see between *Common Sense* and the first *Crisis* essay?

2. How did Paine explain the series of defeats the American army had suffered during the first year of the war?

3. What regional differences among Americans did Paine describe? What, in Paine's opinion, were the differences between American patriots and Tories?

Selected Bibliography

Aldridge, Alfred Owen. *Man of Reason: The Life of Thomas Paine*. Philadelphia, 1959.

————. *Thomas Paine's American Ideology*. Newark, Del., 1984.

Ayer, A. J. *Thomas Paine*. London, 1988.

Conway, Moncure Daniel. *The Life of Thomas Paine*. 2 vols. New York, 1893.

————, ed. *The Writings of Thomas Paine*. 2 vols. New York, 1894.

Foner, Eric. *Tom Paine and Revolutionary America*. New York, 1976.

————, ed. *Thomas Paine: Collected Writings*. New York, 1995.

Foner, Philip S., ed. *The Complete Writings of Thomas Paine*. 2 vols. New York, 1945.

Fruchtman, Jack. *Thomas Paine: Apostle of Freedom*. New York, 1994.

Gimbel, Richard. *Thomas Paine: A Bibliographical Check List of* Common Sense *with an Account of its Publication*. New Haven, 1956.

Keane, John. *Tom Paine: A Political Life*. Boston, 1995.

Oldys, Francis [George Chalmers]. *The Life of Thomas Pain*. London, 1791.

Smith, Olivia. *The Politics of Language, 1791–1819*. Oxford, 1984.

Williamson, Audrey. *Thomas Paine: His Life, Work, and Times*. New York, 1974.

Index